BATTLE FOR THE SKIES

BLITZ EDITIONS

Published by Blitz Editions
an imprint of Bookmart Ltd
Registered Number 2372865
Trading as Bookmart Ltd
Desford Road
Enderby
Leicester LE9 5AD

ISBN 1 85605 264 8

This material has previously appeared in *Witness to World War II.*

PICTURE CREDITS
The publisher would like to thank the following organisations for supplying photographs for use in this book.
Every effort has been made to contact the copyright holders for the pictures. In some cases they have been untraceable, for which we offer our apologies.

Imperial War Museum; Bundesarchiv; Bibliothek fur Zeitgeschechte; J Baker Collection; Biggin Hill Archives; Stato Maggiore Aeronautica; RAF Museum; Robert Hunt Library; Musee d'Histoire Contemporaine; The Boeing Co. Archives; USAF Photo Section; Renault; VSEL Vickers; Los Alamos Scientific Lab; US Navy Photo Section.

THE AUTHOR

Karen Farrington is a writer and former Fleet Street journalist who has specialised in the study of conflict throughout the 20th Century. In compiling Witness to World War II she has personally interviewed scores of veterans from around the world, obtaining a unique insight into the war through the eyes of the men on the front line. Among her previous books is 'Fated Destiny', an historical pot pourri of the curious, shocking and mysterious which includes accounts of some of the greatest military blunders in recent history. Karen Farrington is married with three children and lives in Exmoor, Devon.

This book was produced by Amazon Publishing Limited
Designed by Wilson Design Associates

Printed in the Czech Republic
51763

Battle for the Skies

BATTLE OF BRITAIN

When France was overrun, Führer Adolf Hitler cast his eyes across the English Channel and set his sights on Britain.

Although he never had an appetite for war with the island, he now saw it as the next jewel in his crown. He even believed its government and people would choose to make peace after the unstoppable power of the Reich had been so amply illustrated in France.

He was, of course, wrong. A peace offer made to Britain in July 1940 was rebuffed – even though the remnants of its army, hounded out of Europe via Dunkirk, were in disarray. Hitler made up his mind to invade and began gathering the necessary invasion forces in the newly acquired Channel ports of Holland, Belgium and France.

Yet while the Germans were veterans of waging attacking wars on land, they had never tackled the sea before. Nor was Germany a great seafaring nation. Hitler believed the necessary arrangements for taking war across the water could be made in a matter of weeks. Given that 'Operation Overlord', carried out from Britain in 1944 to free France, took upwards of a year to plan, he was woefully shortsighted.

Göring pledged to the Führer that the Royal Air Force would be banished forever

The effectiveness or otherwise of his plan was never revealed, however. For it was clear even to the buoyant Hitler that an invasion could not go ahead until his air force had charge of the skies. It was one of the few issues that united his warring chiefs of staff, too.

'The British Air Force must be eliminated to such an extent that it will be incapable of putting up any substantial opposition to the invading troops,' Hitler told his generals. Göring, the supremo of German air power, was all ears. He blithely pledged to the Führer that the Royal Air Force would be banished forever.

IN EASY REACH

On paper, it seemed Göring had good reason to be confident. The Luftwaffe had a three-to-one numerical superiority against the RAF which had lost nearly half its strength during the Battle of France. German pilots were experienced, having flown missions throughout the Spanish Civil War as well as the more recent hostilities. Now they were installed in airfields in France, the Low Countries and Norway, within easy reach of Britain.

Göring believed his men would smash the Royal Air Force in much the same way as they had destroyed the Polish and French air forces before.

'Operation Sealion', Hitler's planned offensive against Britain which would bear him triumphantly to London, was set for 15 September 1940. The German navy chief Admiral Raeder had convinced Hitler his forces could not be prepared any sooner. Nor could it happen much later than that for fear of the invasion force falling foul of autumn storms.

Timing was crucial – but this did not unduly concern the Luftwaffe

Left: **Spitfires like this one proved the saviours of Britain.**
Top right: **Göring was confident his Luftwaffe aircraft could finish the RAF.**
Right: **Air crews were scrambled at a moment's notice when attacks came.**

Top: **Formations of Messerschmitt 110s became a familiar sight in the skies.**
Above: **Britain and the Commonwealth countries were recruiting air crews.**

chief, who was still smarting at the way the British Expeditionary Force had escaped from the French coast under his nose. When the Luftwaffe began its operations against Britain in July, Göring was sure he had time enough to fulfill his part of the bargain. Privately, he thought four days would be sufficient to virtually annihilate his opposition. Events proved his optimism to be wildly misplaced.

For its part, Britain waited in anticipation during the summer of 1940 for the start of a battle for its very existence. Air reconnaissance teams spotted the gathering German forces. Hitler's intentions were clear.

Many of the men plucked from the beach at Dunkirk were redeployed on coastal defences. The Royal Navy played its part by attacking the collection of landing craft mushrooming at the occupied ports. Airmen joined the action and laid still more mines in the Channel to hamper a seaborne force destined for Britain.

There was a new evacuation among the children of London and the south east. As tension and expectation mounted on the home front, production doubled during June in factories working round-the-clock in a bid to help Britain's defenders meet the foe on equal terms. Lord Beaverbrook, minister of aircraft production, appealed to the public to donate its metal scrap to build fighters. The result was mountains of old iron which could never be transformed into Spitfires or Hurricanes. But in terms of a morale-boosting exercise, it was a runaway success.

CONVOYS ATTACKED

As the German victory parades and celebrations died down in France there came the opening salvos of the Battle of Britain. They were quite tame affairs by comparison with what was to come, a bid to 'soften up' Britain. The targets were Britain's lifeline convoys as they reached home waters and the coastal ports, most notably Portsmouth and Dover. Both sides suffered losses in the air, with the English pilots, ground controllers and radar operators learning some valuable lessons.

Lord Beaverbrook appealed to the public to donate its metal scrap to build fighters

Germany had begun with about 2,600 aircraft ready for action. They were in the main Messerschmitt fighters and Dornier, Heinkel, and Junkers bombers. They were well-organised into groups – Luftflotte 2 flew from Belgium, Luftflotte 3 from northern France, and Luftflotte 5 was based in either Norway or Denmark.

FIGHTER COMMAND

Lining up against them were fewer than 700 operational aircraft for the Royal Air Force. There were the legendary Spitfires and Hurricanes and some outdated Blenheim bombers.

Britain's aerial defences were divided into four groups. Fighter Command 10 Group covered south west England, Fighter Command 11 Group oversaw the south east including London, Fighter Command 12

FINEST HOUR

'Let us brace ourselves to our duty and so bear ourselves that if the British Commonwealth and Empire lasts a thousand years men will still say, "This was their finest hour".'

(Winston Churchill after the fall of France.)

In the middle of August Göring opened phase two of the Battle of Britain

Irish, seven Americans, two Rhodesians, one Jamaican and a Palestinian.

Now Germany was down by some 217 planes. The losses by Fighter Command were fewer than 100 but its outlook was bleaker than that of the enemy. British aircraft reserves were tiny. Yet it was the loss of experienced pilots either by death or injury that began to concern Air Chief Marshal Sir Hugh Dowding most. Despite the acute pressure of his position, Dowding, a master tactician, did a first-class job of keeping the marauding German planes at bay during those hectic months of summer and autumn 1940. Yet Churchill unceremoniously replaced him once the threat of 'Operation Sealion' had passed.

Above: **Göring and his staff officers survey England across the Channel, convinced the island would easily fall.**

Group patrolled the airspace over the Midlands, while Fighter Command 13 Group was based in northern England and Scotland.

Britain was not standing entirely alone, as the line-up for the ensuing battle proved. Although more than 2,500 of the men who took part were British, there were also 147 Poles, 101 New Zealanders, 94 Canadians, 87 Czechs, 29 Belgians, 22 South Africans, 22 Australians, 14 Free French, ten

In the middle of August, Göring opened phase two of the Battle of Britain. His target now was RAF Fighter Command itself. Daily attacks were made on the airfields of southern England. Unlike the unfortunate air forces of crushed Allies Poland and France, the British planes

Left: Air crews at Biggin Hill, Kent, enjoy a few moments' respite.

Below: Despite the dangers, pilots and crews always appeared relaxed.

were not caught on the ground. Britain's radar system, the most advanced in the world, gave early warning after seeing incoming formations of enemy bombers. There was just enough time to scramble the pilots and bring the valuable men and planes into the air.

Smoke from planes embroiled in dog-fights was scrawled across the sky

For now the heroes of the battle were the ground crews. It was their job to patch up not only the planes which were battered during aerial spats but also the hangars and runways damaged by bombs, to keep the Royal Air Force working.

Göring earmarked 13 August as 'Eagle Day' when a preponderance of German planes would swarm over the British skies and finally subjugate the stubborn RAF. Despite wave upon wave of Luftwaffe planes, his plan failed. Smoke from planes embroiled in dog-fights was scrawled across the sky. The British fighters held their own.

NIMBLE SPITFIRES

German bombers were at a disadvantage against the nimble Spitfires. Laden with bombs, they were no match for the British planes. But the RAF fighters were constantly struggling to achieve the best height and position to carry out attacks on the German formations as they crossed into Britain. Not wishing to waste vital manpower and resources, ground control never scrambled pilots until the last moment when they were sure a raid was imminent. It gave them little time to plan the most effective attack.

Both sides fell victim to erroneous propaganda. The RAF airmen were buoyed to hear that German air force losses were running at three or four times their own. In fact, vastly inflated German casualty figures were broadcast, some of which were not rectified until after the war. Göring, meanwhile, was happily convinced during the early stages of the Battle of Britain that many airfields were out of action and scores of British planes were destroyed, estimates which were grossly exaggerated.

On 15 August nearly 1,800 sorties were flown by the German airmen,

BATTLE OF BRITAIN

In the Battle of Britain, RAF Fighter Command was divided into groups distributed throughout the country. The south west of England was the responsibility of 10 Group, London and the south east was covered by 11 Group, the Midlands region was patrolled by 12 Group, northern England and Scotland was the beat of 13 Group. Against these forces were three Luftwaffe formations – Luftflotte 2, Luftflotte 3 and Luftflotte 5.

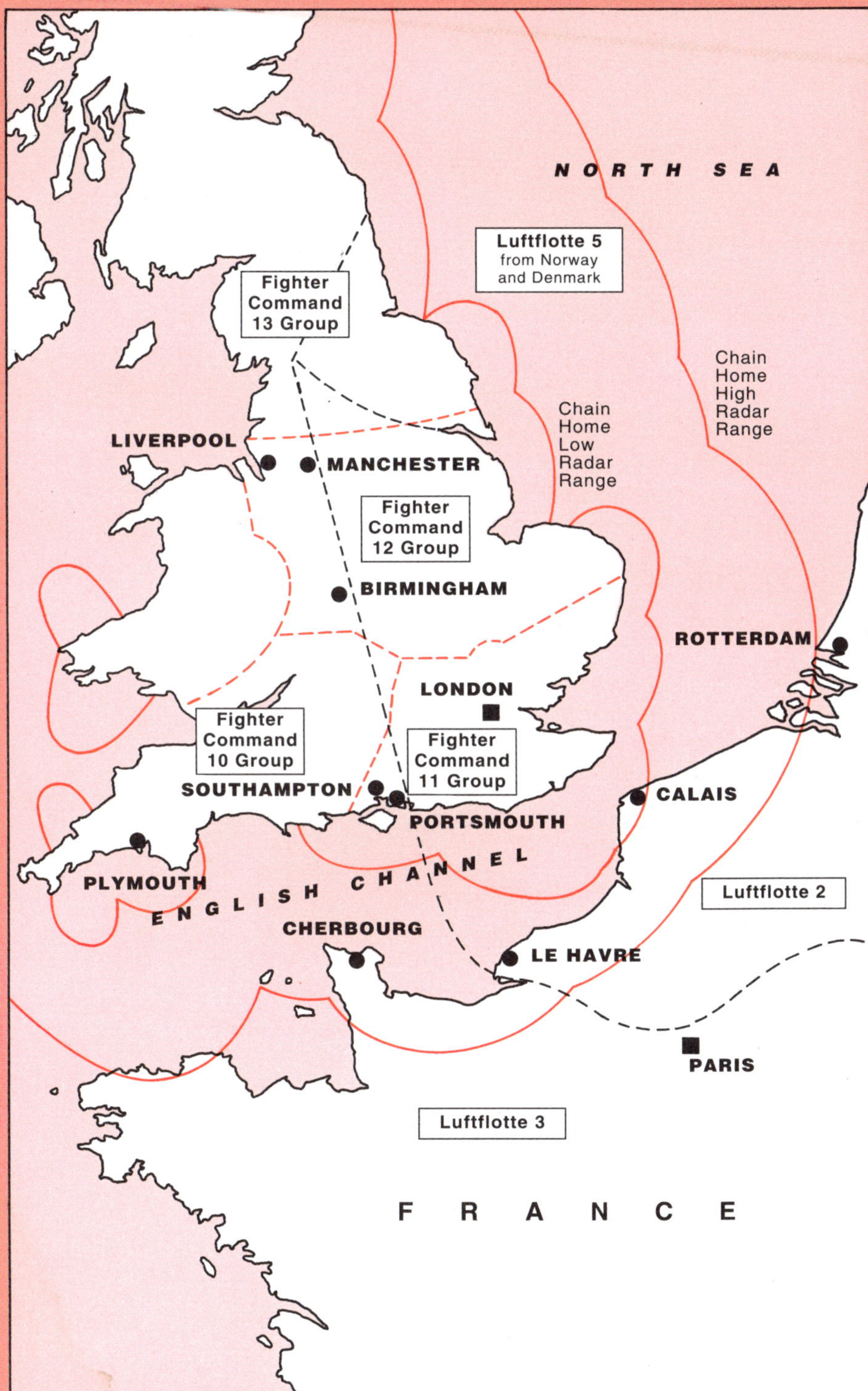

attacking targets from Newcastle to Hampshire. Britain was forewarned by radar, and each flight was attacked from the ground and the air and there were 75 German losses against Britain's 34.

The following day 1,700 sorties were made over Britain, with Göring confident the RAF would be left in tatters. Yet on that day and on many days to come, the German pilots found themselves confronted with healthy numbers of British planes and pilots.

Göring was left fuming at the apparent inability of his men to finish off the RAF. In addition, he was counting the cost of 363 lost aircraft and crew.

Above: **A Heinkel 111 over the Thames, taken from another German plane.**

Of course, the incessant demands on each and every British squadron were causing immense difficulties by mid-August. Britain had lost 181 fighters in the air and 30 more on the ground. Only 170 replacement aircraft had thus far been manufactured, while just 63 new pilots had been brought up to replace the 154

Left: **Temple Underground station doubled as an air-raid shelter during the Blitz.**

lost in battle. The raiders had succeeded in knocking out a radar station at Ventnor on the Isle of Wight, which was a serious blow, although their main aim of wrecking airfields had been frustrated. How long could the casual, seemingly cheery young men in silk scarves and leather jackets who laid their lives on the line several times a day without an outward trace of anxiety hold out?

Dowding, by skilful management, contained the mounting problems. Yet he was wearied by the effort and certain in the knowledge that Fighter Command could not cope with many more all-out raids. Another change in German tack saved the force from certain defeat.

Stage three of the Battle of Britain was sparked in part by accident. On 23 August a German pilot ditched his bombs over London, not to cause mayhem in the capital but rather to speed his flight home. Churchill was outraged. In retaliation, he ordered the bombing of the German capital, Berlin.

Now it was Hitler's turn to be furious. He pledged in turn to annihilate London, abandoning his deeply held wish to occupy the city unscarred by bomb damage. With the German campaign to obliterate the RAF clearly failing, he thought it was time for a new and different tactic. The wholesale bombing of London would not only hit at the heart of the British government but would demoralise its people. 'Sealion', he believed, would still go ahead as planned. The gloves were now off. It was the start of an arduous period of bombing raids which would test the strength of the RAF and also the people of Britain to the very limit.

Below: **The unmistakeable shape of St Paul's cathedral stands firm among the bomb damage in the City of London.**

Now the German forces were throwing their entire weight at Britain. With their losses amounting to 60 planes on 15 September, the decision to undertake mostly night bombing raids was made.

Searchlights in London were unable to track the fast-moving attackers. Night fighters in the RAF squadrons badly needed airborne interception radar to hit back, which took valuable time to provide. The demands on the men of the RAF, already weary from their exertions, were enormous, and their ability to strike back under cover of darkness was limited. They were sleeping for just a few hours in every 24 before being scrambled once more. The casualties among them continued to mount and, for the first time, their losses exceeded those of the enemy.

◆ EYE WITNESS ◆

Fred Graves, of Swindon, Wiltshire, served in the RAF ground crews which worked on Hurricanes and Spitfires during the Battle of Britain. Later in the war he serviced Lancasters of Bomber Command and was based near Newmarket.

'I remember the Battle of Britain as a non-stop series of dog-fights in the skies above us. Our pilots knew they had a very low life expectancy. I lost an awful lot of friends.

I was particularly impressed by the Polish airmen serving with us. Every time there was a scramble alert they would race out, usually still in their shirt sleeves, jump into a plane and take off. They were very highly motivated to hit back at Germany.

Airmen rarely if ever showed they were scared. Even the Lancaster bomber crews assigned to missions over the Ruhr somehow coped with the pressure. You could detect a reluctance among them – simply because the Ruhr industrial region was so heavily defended – but they did their duty.

I think teamwork helped beat the fear. Bomber air crews were teams. If one of them wasn't fit or well then the whole crew was grounded until he was. They also had to have faith in their aircraft and in us as ground crew. We were the last friendly faces they saw before they flew east.

Looking back it is a miracle some of these men ever made it home. Their aircraft were so shot up they were almost unrecognisable.'

It took hours, sometimes days, to find bodies trapped in their wrecked homes

Meanwhile, on the ground, the conditions for residents of London and, eventually, other main British cities were appalling.

The London docks were among the first targets in a daring daylight attack on 7 September. Nearby residents watched in horror as scores of German bombers sparked a ferocious blaze. It took just an hour for the Luftwaffe to drop 300 tons of high explosives and countless numbers of incendiaries. Hours later several hundred more bombers returned.

At night the raging fires burned like beacons, guiding Luftwaffe pilots to their target.

Before very long, London Underground stations became shelters for frightened city folk despite an immediate ban on such a use. People slept end to end in close proximity to friends, neighbours and complete strangers. Those lucky enough to have gardens and shelters in their gardens became accustomed to retiring to them in time for tea and staying put until daybreak. It was soon clear that the option of sheltering under a sturdy wooden table was not an inspired choice as house after house was reduced to rubble by the bombs.

It took hours, sometimes days, to find bodies trapped in their wrecked homes. There was trial by fire as intense blazes raged. If bombs had failed to explode, there was continuing danger for the residents and workers of London even after the planes were long gone.

On the ground fire-watchers, full-time firefighters and auxiliaries, air raid precaution wardens and the Home Guard did their best to combat the terrible ravages of the raids.

***Above:* Coventry was blitzed in a raid code-named 'Moonlight Sonata'. The raid claimed 568 lives.**

Despite all this, the mood in London was far from one of defeatism. The spin-off planned by Hitler of grinding the British public into the ground with the incessant bombing raids was failing miserably. In the tube stations there was impromptu entertainment from singers and musicians. Cups of tea were passed around and soon people learned to pay little heed to the sound of pounding bombs above.

BUSINESS AS USUAL

Instead of people weeping and wailing on the streets when the harsh light of day revealed the full extent of the night raids, there was a camaraderie which no one could have foreseen. Business went on as usual in daylight hours, despite shattered windows, fractured gas and water pipes and the unnerving sight of double-decker buses upturned in bomb craters. The spirit of the people of London was ultimately symbolised in the great cathedral of St Pauls, which stood intact overlooking the battered city while smoke from incendiary fires plumed around its dome.

If anyone was demoralised by the successive and apparently fruitless attacks it was the German pilots who were patently failing in their task of bringing Britain to its knees.

The attacks came in earnest from 15 September as Göring tried to ground the British air force in time for 'Sealion'. That day a record 56 Luftwaffe planes were brought down. Hitler twice postponed making a final decision on whether or not to go ahead before making his decision day 17 September. As the day dawned, London was smoking. But the Luftwaffe had paid a heavy price for the privilege of setting alight this historic capital, and the planes of the Royal Air Force were not only still challenging their fighters but also found time to bombard the Channel ports where the German invasion fleet was based.

HItler had no option but to call off 'Sealion' indefinitely

Hitler had no option but to call off 'Sealion' indefinitely. The Battle of Britain was won and the stout little island was safe from invasion. That meant renewed hope for occupied Europe, for without Britain from which to mount an attack on Hitler's Nazi empire there would have been barely a flicker of opportunity for liberation. Churchill's words of praise and thanks for the gallant RAF, spoken back in August, echoed through the free world. 'Never in the field of human conflict was so much owed by so many to so few.'

Yet the ordeal went on for both the men of the RAF and the people of Britain. Luftwaffe attacks continued unabated. London was attacked for 76 nights in succession and failed to enjoy much more than a few hours of eerie peace until the middle of 1941.

Anti-aircraft guns boomed in answer to the rain of bombs. There was little chance of them hitting their target. Only 75 aircraft were brought down by anti-aircraft shells – when the Luftwaffe flew about 12,000

THE FEW

'Never in the field of human conflict was so much owed by so many to so few.'

(Winston Churchill after the Battle of Britain.)

RUDOLPH HESS

The Führer flew into a three-day rage when his deputy, Rudolph Walter Richard Hess, flew to Britain to make peace. A full day after the flight from Germany in a Messerschmitt 110 fighter aircraft, German radio explained away the demoralising desertion by claiming Hess was suffering from hallucinations.

British intelligence chiefs, meanwhile, were similarly at a loss to know what to make of the ace pilot who had been a loyal member of the Nazi party since 1920. On 10 May 1941, when he came down to earth at the end of a parachute and suffered a broken ankle, he claimed he had an important message for the Duke of Hamilton. This message was, apparently, a peace formula which would end the conflict between Britain and Germany.

High-ranking British officers and Churchill himself would not hear of making peace by the back door. Nevertheless, they were reluctant to trumpet the capture of such a key Nazi. Were they being duped by Hitler? Was there a further dimension to this unexpected prize which had fallen into their laps?

Even today, no one can tell whether Hess was demented at the scale of the bloodshed and hatched his plan to end the war accordingly; whether he discussed the plan with Hitler who wished to secure peace with Britain before invading Russia; or whether it was in fact the real Hess who carried out the madcap caper. Years later there were claims that the man held by the Allies was in fact an imposter, dispatched by Himmler or Göring after the murder of Hess.

What remains certain is that the man who fell to earth that night in 1941 was tried as a war criminal at Nuremberg, sentenced to life imprisonment and incarcerated at Spandau prison in Germany for 46 years until his death, apparently by suicide.

sorties over Britain. Post-war investigation proved that for every bomber shot down by an anti-aircraft gun in September 1940 the gun had to expend an enormous 20,000 rounds. Results did improve and by February 1941 the figure was down to 3,000. Still, the knowledge that something was being done was at least a small comfort to the population.

Göring also turned his attention to other British cities. Perhaps his aim was to eliminate great industrial centres and not simply to mete out punishment to British civilians. In fact, the lack of accuracy among bombers of the age ensured that civilians were foremost among the casualties.

In Coventry, 568 people were killed on 14 November 1940 when German bombers opened their doors and let 450 tons of bombs drop on the city. Its historic cathedral was ruined. Birmingham, Manchester, Exeter, Sheffield, Liverpool, Cardiff, Swansea, Bath, Plymouth, Ipswich, Norwich, Southampton, Sunderland, Hull, Middlesborough and Canterbury all also received a battering.

BITTER TRUTH

Countless thousands of people were made homeless by these air raids, being left only with the clothes they stood up in. During the worst of them which occurred in December 1940 and May 1941 in London, the firefighters ran out of water as they fought hundreds of blazes and were left with little option but to let them rage on. On 10 May 1941 550 German bombers unleashed 700 tons of high explosives and thousands of incendiaries, killing 1,436 people and destroying 700 acres of city. Just 14 of the attackers were brought down.

From August 1940 to May 1941, 44,000 civilians died and 103,000 were injured. The bitter truth was that the destruction and misery was no precursor to an invasion of Britain. It was merely a camouflage for Hitler's real intentions, to expand eastwards across the Russian borders, to Moscow and beyond. Only when Luftwaffe planes were pulled out of France to concentrate on the Russian front did the attacks on Britain subside.

From August 1940 to May 1941, 44,000 civilians died

Left: **As dawn breaks, the destruction of the previous night's raid on London's docklands is revealed.**

AIR BATTLE – BALKANS

Both Axis and Allied powers saw benefit in opening a battle-front in the Balkans.

For Hitler, there was a chance of mopping up a potentially troublesome southern flank before mounting 'Operation Barbarossa', the invasion of Russia.

Churchill and his top brass saw a successful campaign in Greece or Yugoslavia offering a possible back-door entry into Germany when no access seemed available at the front.

In the event, the short and bloody campaign in the region left both sides as losers when it illustrated both the advantages – and drawbacks – of an airborne campaign.

Mussolini had opened hostilities when he invaded Greece on 28 October 1940. It was an impetuous decision which he lived to regret. Not only did it infuriate his ally Hitler, who had fostered an amenable relationship with Greece's ruler General Metaxas and considered the country in the bag. But it served to further humiliate Mussolini and his troops in addition to their inept showing in North and East Africa.

For the Greeks, although poorly equipped for modern warfare, were imbued with fighting spirit and managed to see off the Italians, pushing them back behind their lines in occupied Albania.

Britain was determined to stand by pledges of aid made to Greece – even though it had been unable to honour promises made to Romania, which was occupied by German troops at the start of October 1940.

ALLIES IN GREECE

Hitler had no option but to intervene in the action. However, for a few months he bided his time.

Having dispatched several thousand men, the British were keen to send even more of their contingent presently in North Africa to the aid of the Greeks. Metaxas was unsure. Although the presence of air support was welcomed, his own men were putting up an adequate performance and the presence of Allied ground troops would only succeed in drawing the awesome firepower of an irate Hitler. Instead of men, he said, he would rather have their boots. His own soldiers were suffering greatly due to the inadequacies of their footwear.

By the end of November 1940 three squadrons of Blenheim bombers and fighters had been stationed in Greece and the numbers continued to increase. Their brief, to defend Athens.

The political outlook changed at the end of January 1941 when Metaxas died suddenly and was replaced by Emmanuel Tsouderos who was well-disposed towards the Allies.

At a meeting in February, it was agreed the 1st Armoured Brigade, the 6th Australian Division and the 2nd New Zealand Division would be stationed in Greece to repel possible German aggression. With Bulgaria to the east rapidly falling under the influence of Germany, and with Italy in the west, the fresh troops could plug defensive gaps left open by the Greeks fighting in Albania. Churchill enjoyed the idea of rescuing the 'cradle of civilisation', as Greece is known, from the clutches of Nazism.

The Greeks were imbued with fighting spirit and managed to see off the Italians

Also feeling the weight of the Nazi jackboot was neighbouring Yugoslavia, a country Britain failed to support. The government, under Prince Regent Paul and Prime Minister Dragisa Cvetkovic, were given an invitation-ultimatum in March 1941. Yugoslavia was to join the Axis powers. Prince Regent Paul was unable to secure aid from the British. With a heavy heart he finally gave his

Far left: **A ship unloading supplies for the Allies in Suda Bay comes to grief.**
Left: **Italian soldiers were held at bay when they tried to invade Greece.**

EYE WITNESS

Howard Ganly was in the US 82nd Airborne Division. He was dropped behind enemy lines before D-Day to act as a pathfinder.

'I was a little bit lost. They gave us the wrong maps. I made a few mistakes. I was shot at by my own men. They had got hold of some farmers' clothes and put them on, thinking they would be good disguises in German territory. Some of them were from my own company. I could have had them court martialled but I didn't. They stuck to me close for the rest of the war.

I was looking for open fields that weren't mined and didn't have big stumps stuck in the ground so they would be suitable for landing gliders. I would signal the gliders if it was OK to come in, with special lights and flares. We didn't dare use radios too much. I was very scared, I was just 19 years old. I came into the service when I was 17. The army kept pushing me around from one place to another. I didn't have any family, I spent most of my childhood in orphan asylums. I joined up to get a job and the money was good.

I survived D-Day but ran into trouble later on in Europe. I baled out in Holland behind enemy lines. A young Dutch girl put me in a barge and hid me from the Germans. She probably saved my life. I looked for her a few times after the war but never found her. I broke my leg and back in the fall. I have been disabled ever since. I was hospitalised for two years. I worked on and off but most of the time I have been crippled up.'

consent and the Tripartite Pact was signed on 25 March.

Fury against the agreement among the Yugoslav people erupted immediately. There was an internal revolt which unseated the prince regent and put 17-year-old King Peter II in his place. On 27 March the pact signed with Hitler was ripped into pieces. The sombre mood which had descended on Belgrade and beyond was suddenly lifted, to be replaced with rejoicing.

HITLER OUTRAGED

The outbreak of anti-Nazism outraged Hitler. He resolved to teach the people of Yugoslavia a lesson. German commanders were told: 'Politically it is especially important that the blow against Yugoslavia is carried out with pitiless harshness.' It made sense to combat the Greek problem at the same time so 'Operation Strafgericht' (punishment) against Yugoslavia and 'Operation Marita' against Greece were co-ordinated to begin on 6 April.

Hitler's campaign to pummel Yugoslavia into submission started with a dawn raid by the Luftwaffe. The sole declaration of war was the shower of bombs which hit Belgrade at 6am. The day-long assault claimed 17,000 lives and the grand buildings of the capital crumbled.

The day closed with another disaster, this time for Greece. The Luftwaffe wreaked havoc on Piraeus, the harbour of the Greek capital, which was crowded with ships from an incoming convoy. As the German bombs rained down destruction, one ship at anchor, SS Glen Fraser, had its 250-ton cargo of explosives ignited by a direct hit. The roaring explosion that followed flattened much of the harbour, sank yet more vessels and even shattered windows in Athens some seven miles distant.

'It is especially important that the blow against Yugoslavia is carried out with pitiless harshness'

German armies began driving into both countries at the usual alarming Panzer pace. Yugoslavia, which had a small army, held out for just 11 days. Much of its air force was knocked out on the ground by Luftwaffe attacks. The inglorious fortnight was compounded when Royal Yugoslav Air Force Hurricanes became

Right: **Germany soon won command of the skies over Greece, and this tipped the balance of the battle in their favour.**

Above: Serbs in Yugoslavia were no friends of the Germans. Many fought as guerrillas against the invaders.

embroiled in a dog-fight over Belgrade with some BF-109s which unfortunately belonged to the very same air force.

RETREAT TO CRETE

The Greek army, too, was having difficulty fending off the advance. The fighting was gruelling. British commander General Sir Henry 'Jumbo' Maitland Wilson soon saw the hopelessness of the situation and ordered an evacuation to the south. On 22 April Greece capitulated also. The initial destination of the fleeing Allied troops was the Peloponnese islands linked to mainland Greece by a bridge at Corinth. Then it was onwards to the island of Crete.

Under fire from the Luftwaffe above, the Royal Navy came in to the southerly beaches on 26 and 27 April to hoist 26,000 men to safety. Left behind were 900 dead, 1,200 wounded and something in the order of 10,000 men who had fallen prisoner to the Germans. Then there was the abandoned weaponry, amounting to more than 100 tanks, 400 guns, 1,800 machine guns and 8,000 vehicles. The RAF had lost more than 200 aircraft in total while the Royal Navy had had two destroyers and about 25 other ships sunk.

On Crete there was chaos with hundreds of leaderless men awaiting an uncertain future

On Crete there was chaos with hundreds of leaderless men awaiting an uncertain future. The only thing of which they could be sure was that Hitler's men would not rest until Crete too fell into their grasp.

In command was Major-General Bernard Freyberg, a pugnacious New Zealander who was ready to refuse the mantle of leadership until he discovered there was a sizeable number of his own men on the island – troops he believed had been taken back to Egypt.

His force amounted to two New Zealand brigades, about 7,750 men, plus an Australian brigade, two further battalions of Australians and a field regiment of artillery, with a combined total of 6,500. There were 15,000 British troops, too, comprising a brigade of infantrymen and part

Above: **A Panzer division parades its might before the centuries-old Acropolis in Athens, after the city was overrun.**

of the 1st Armoured Brigade, complete with two light tanks. Also at his disposal were about 10,000 Greeks. The Allies also had the support of the local population, many of whom would take up arms against the incoming Germans.

Freyberg, who won the VC in World War I, set about defending the island as best he could. He focused his forces at the three airfields, Maleme, Retimo and Heraklion, and the easily accessible Suda Bay.

From North Africa he received some tanks – less than two dozen but welcome nonetheless – and some rather war-worn artillery. There was a further injection of men, the 2nd Leicesters, who arrived on 16 May.

Crete – 136 miles long and an uneven 40 miles wide, and full of mountainous terrain – could hardly be adequately defended given the small number of men. Yet Freyberg was determined his men would give it their best shot.

From North Africa Freyberg received some tanks – less than two dozen but welcome

For Germany, the invasion of Crete posed some difficulties, not least in how to transport troops to the island. The Royal Navy had established a command of the seas. Already the shortcomings of the Italian navy had been shown up and the German command did not trust its ally's sailors with the lives of crack soldiers of the Third Reich. So an all-out amphibious assault was deemed too dangerous.

Yet in the air the Luftwaffe was unrivalled. By 18 May only seven RAF aircraft were left on Crete, and these were promptly withdrawn to Egypt. An airborne assault might work. Airborne forces had been in existence since 1927 when the first was formed by Italy. The Soviet Union soon followed suit and the value of these sky-fliers was clear. They could be dropped into enemy territory either in small numbers for the purpose of sabotage or in large numbers to begin an invasion.

◆ EYE WITNESS ◆

Morley Pence, 71, from Los Angeles, served with the 26 Mobile Reclamation Squad of the 442 Troop Carrier Command. Based at Thatcham, near Reading, he built and tested CG4A canvas and wood gliders (capable of carrying six men or two men and a Jeep) for 'Operation Overlord'.

❛ Before the invasion the whole of southern England was one big military camp. Everything was either painted green or under green canvas. It was like the civilians had all left for the summer.

It was such an unreal time. I remember us bringing aeroplanes through the centre of London on 40ft flat-bed trucks. There was absolutely no room for us to get round the corners so we just made room. No one seemed to mind. Actually, no one seemed to even notice.

When I see London now, this huge, busy bustling city, it brings it all back. I marvel at how the hell we drove those trucks anywhere. ❜

There were, of course, numerous hazards inherent in airborne operations, but until now the Germans had known only successes. Their use of paratroopers in Norway, Belgium and Holland during 1940 had brought striking results. The 55 men from the 'Granite' assault team who parachuted into Eben Emael, the strongest fortress in the world, on the Belgian-Dutch border, in May of that year, defeated 700 defenders in less than a day.

The use of paratroopers in Norway, Belgium and Holland during 1940 had brought striking results

The Luftwaffe's airborne supremo was Kurt Student, a World War I fighter pilot and squadron leader. He had keenly studied the potential of airborne techniques in Russia during the 1930s and saw 'Blitzkreig' as an excellent opportunity to put theory into practice.

Not only did he have troops leaping from flying aircraft but also equipment-bearing soldiers carried in gliders, and 'air mobile' forces, men trained in the art of going into action straight from the door of a landed plane. He sought to use all types in the invasion of Crete.

'MERKUR'

'Operation Merkur', the German attack on Crete, was to be launched following days of heavy aerial bombardment, with the landing of 36 gliders whose elite troops would knock out anti-aircraft guns and capture key locations.

The men of XI Air Corps' 1st Assault Regiment were the next penned in to see action, capturing an airfield and other key locations. At the same time, men of the 3rd Parachute Regiment would drop further up the coast and the aim was for both prongs to battle to a reunion.

Then a second wave was planned in which the 1st and 2nd Parachute Regiments were introduced with heavier arms, while two further battalions arrived by sea in fast motor-cutters. More amphibious activity was planned when the island was in German control. First hitch for the Germans came when too few planes were provided, forcing the commanders to cut the size of the airborne assault.

Student and his men believed only a few thousand men would be there to meet them when the attack on 20 May got underway. It was a catastrophic miscalculation.

As a swarm of aircraft receded into the distance, hundreds of parachutes billowed in the breeze. The troops on the ground had plenty of time to take aim and fire, relishing a chance to get revenge on the men who had so recently chased them out of Greece. The helpless paras were picked off one by one as they all fell

Right: **General Kurt Student was the mastermind behind German paratroopers' triumphs – and their failures, like the ill-fated assault on Crete.**

Above: **German paratroopers were confident as they embarked for Crete, with good reason. Until then, they had only known success.**

virtually on top of the defending Anzac and British forces. Olive groves and rocky escarpments were littered with bodies, many still strapped into 'chutes.

Some parachutists didn't even make it out of their planes. Ground fire penetrated the hulls of the low-flying aircraft, killing or wounding men while they were still inside.

The few that survived were compelled to seek cover and join up with their comrades as soon as they could. Only those who dropped away from their targets – and thus away from defensive fire – escaped being cut down. It was for them to fight their way across the rocky landscape and unite with other groups.

Communications were poor on both sides. With telephone lines down and radios suffering patchy reception, the Allied groups felt equally isolated from assistance and exposed to the enemy. It caused one New Zealand commander to withdraw his men from a commanding position in the heights above an airfield, leaving a vital foothold open to the attackers.

Groves and escarpments were littered with bodies, many still strapped into their 'chutes

There followed more of the bitter fighting, often at close quarters, with many Allied soldiers claiming victims at the point of a bayonet. Both sides vied for the airfields. There was an uncomfortable stalemate as both Allied and German commanders tried to land reinforcements. The Royal Navy sank the German transports while the Luftwaffe holed the British ships.

GERMAN VICTORY

At Maleme airfield under a barrage of crossfire, brave German pilots began to land their transport planes, some coming to grief on the runway, others colliding with planes that had preceded them. Inside were well-trained, well-armed soldiers fresh and ready for the fight.

The New Zealanders at Maleme were finally overwhelmed. Germany had scored the first victory in the battle for Crete.

And it was a key triumph, for now that the attacking troops had control of Maleme airfield, the gateway was open for supplies and still more troops to be transported in.

OTTO SKORZENY

A scar-faced German captain called Otto Skorzeny was the action-man asked by Hitler to rescue Mussolini from imprisonment in September 1943. Skorzeny, who was frustrated in earlier plans to snatch the Duce to safety by the diligence of the Italian authorities who kept their prized prisoner on the move, planned for a German plane to land on a precarious mountain plateau while he in the company of other troops parachuted into the hotel hideaway where Mussolini was held. Italian guards at the mountain village of Assergi abided by his requests not to resist the bold German move. Mussolini was flown off in the tiny plane which battled to ascend from the plateau. On reaching Rome he was transferred to a Heinkel 111 for a flight to the safety of Vienna.

In less than a week, Freyberg assessed the situation as hopeless. He ordered the Allied troops, by now mentally and physically exhausted, to withdraw to the south where an evacuation was being launched by the Royal Navy.

Between 27 May and 31 May, about 16,500 Allied men were taken off Crete. Germany had sealed its Balkan front.

BALANCE SHEET

Both sides were left counting the cost, however. Left on Crete were 1,750 Allied soldiers killed in action, two thirds of them Anzacs, and 13,500 men now held as prisoners of war. The Royal Navy lost three cruisers and six destroyers in the rescue bid, along with about 2,000 sailors killed or taken prisoner. Also left behind were Greek, British and Anzac soldiers who turned guerrilla to fight a cloaked campaign against the occupiers. It was another inglorious rout for the Allies.

As for the Germans, nearly half the initial force were killed on Crete, amounting to some 3,700 men. Among them were high-ranking officers including a divisional commander, and a colonel. The number of aircraft shot to smithereens by the Allies or junked on the island airstrips was also immense.

Hitler surveyed the results – and decided the price was unacceptably high. Matter-of-factly, he told Student afterwards: 'Of course you know, General, that we shall never do another airborne operation. Crete proved that the days of parachute troops are over.'

It was a gross over-exaggeration. Germany continued to employ parachute troops although never again in such vast numbers. Nevertheless, Hitler did decide to abandon plans to parachute men into Malta, the stepping-stone island in the Mediterranean. Had he won Malta, Hitler might have found victory in the North African campaign, and pushed into the Middle East and India to join hands with Germany's ally Japan.

The Allies observed the German experience on Crete but also decided in favour of using airborne troops in future engagements. Paratroopers played a pivotal role in the success of the D-Day operations in 1944. Theirs was a precarious job, dropping behind enemy lines in darkness to act as pathfinders for the incoming gliders. Men of the US 82nd and 101st Airborne Divisions were also charged with hindering the enemy advance towards to the coast. But the landings did not go as planned.

'Of course you know, General, that we shall never do another airborne operation'

A combination of inexperienced piloting and mistakes in navigation had the men dispersed over a huge

Right: **Captured Australian servicemen are a source of curiosity for their German guards.**

Left: **'Pathfinder' parachutists are briefed before dropping into France, their task to direct airborne forces to landing points.**

were thrown into confusion by the unexpected and unseen troops. One regiment in the 82nd Airborne Division managed to capture the town of Ste Mère Eglise.

British airborne troops were also seeing action as they seized vital bridges and knocked out a battery of guns aimed at the coast. For the British paratroopers, the ultimate test of endurance was to come later in the year at Arnhem in 'Operation Market Garden'.

Montgomery was eager to persuade Eisenhower of the wisdom

area instead of being in a concentrated group. Parachutists found themselves landing in some of the many engorged rivers in the region. Weighed down by their equipment they floundered for hours trying to get out. Others drowned in the struggle. It meant both Divisions were literally thousands of men short

Weighed down by their equipment they floundered for hours trying to get out

when they went into action. All the hazards of airborne operations, particularly those carried out at night, appeared to be coming in at the Americans.

Yet success bred out of disaster. Undoubtedly, the German defenders

Right: **Horsa gliders lie in pieces after landing men in northern France in 1944. On these gliders the fuselage is split from the wings to unload.**

ALLIED SUCCESS

Air superiority during D-Day became the key to Allied success. While it was thought that the Luftwaffe would sent up some 900 aircraft to make 1,200 sorties on D-Day, in fact only 100 were made in daylight and a further 175 after dark. By contrast the RAF alone flew 5,656 sorties on D-Day, about 40 per cent of the total made by the Allies.

Allied aircraft dropped a total of 4,310 paratroops and towed gliders containing 493 men, 17 guns, 44 Jeeps and 55 motorcycles without suffering harassment from enemy bombers.

As well as protecting troops and ships, Allied aircraft dropped 5,267 bombs against the coastal gun batteries.

The first German plane to fall victim on D-Day was a Ju 88, brought down by New Zealand Flying Officer Johnnie Houlton, one of 2,000 pilots in the Second Tactical Air Force who was in a Spitfire.

In the months which followed, three times as many bombs were dropped on Germany than in all the previous years.

of committing the ground troops to one hammer-blow into northern Germany. Eisenhower favoured a fan-shaped attack instead.

'MARKET GARDEN'

'Operation Market Garden' was designed to capture key bridges in Holland through which Allied troops could be funnelled into Germany. The US 101st Airborne Division was charged with gaining land north of Eindhoven, the US 82nd Airborne Division was allocated two big bridges over the Meuse and the Wall rivers, while the British 1st Airborne Division had to seize bridges over the lower Rhine at Arnhem.

The men were carried to their targets in a total of 1,068 aircraft and 478 gliders. While the Americans experienced considerable success on their fronts, the British met enormous German resistance en route to their target. Just one battalion, the 2nd, reached the bridge at Arnhem. Soon after, they were cut off.

Unfortunately for the British paratroopers, the Germans picked Arnhem as a focal point of defence and reinforced their lines with troops, including an SS Panzer corps containing two armoured divisions. All efforts by the British to reach the men isolated at Arnhem were repelled after fierce clashes.

At the bridge, the paratroopers were pushed back into a defensive margin. It took nine days for the men to establish an escape route across the Rhine. Just 2,200 men got out from a force which began with a strength of 10,000. Montgomery's plan to by-pass Germany's defensive Siegfried line had failed. The thrust continued as before.

It took nine days for the men to establish an escape route across the Rhine

Right: **Troops taken by gliders into Arnhem in a bid to short-circuit the route to Berlin. The Britons had a grim fate in store.**

WINGS OVER THE DESERT

The Western Desert Air Force was officially born on 9 October 1940 at Maaton Bagush in North Africa.

Here in the African desert, the theories of modern air warfare were established. For it was in North Africa that the principles of 'partnership' between air, sea and land forces were tried and tested for the first time, helping to put an end to decades of overt inter-service rivalry.

Above: Mussolini believed his air force could win the skies over Africa. Left: Stalwart Beaufighters played a key role in the North African campaign.

Co-operation of the kind enjoyed by air, sea and naval personnel among the Allies was unthinkable for their German and Italian counterparts, who not only fought a common enemy but were constantly embroiled in sniping against different factions on their own side. Indeed, there were plenty of hiccoughs along the way among the Allies with soldiers convinced the only worthwhile aeroplane was the one that flew protectively above their heads, regardless of the risk to the pilot and his inability to achieve results from that vulnerable spot.

The initial trials of tactical airborne operations were honed by the men of the Desert Air Force until they finally became adopted everywhere.

Unfortunately for the Italians, early promise was soon done down by the Desert Air Force

Lessons learned in the Desert Air Force now seem rudimentary and even naive. Yet aerial combat was still in its infancy when the war commenced. Fliers in World War I had the opportunity to make only elementary trials and errors. Little was done to advance the theory of warfare in the air after 1918 as most nations were concentrating on peace. And until the conflict in the desert got underway, the Royal Air Force was from necessity concentrating primarily on defence.

To call it simply a Desert Air Force is to vastly over-simplify the case. The men who worked under its umbrella saw action in the skies above Egypt, Libya, East and West Africa, Greece, Yugoslavia, Palestine, Italy and other hot spots in the region.

This tremendous fighting force grew from an original nucleus of some 29 squadrons – a total of 600 aircraft. These were all that were available to Middle East commander Air Chief Marshal Sir Arthur Longmore when hostilities with Italy commenced in 1940. Included in this total were a goodly number of outdated biplanes and obsolete Blenheim bombers. That summer on the home front saw the Battle of Britain reach its momentous heights. So the chances of getting top-notch replacements were slim.

In addition, the airmen faced the same shortages that cursed the soldiers on the ground, those of water, fuel and spare parts to replace those worn by the inhospitable terrain.

Against them was the might of the Regia Aeronautica, the Italian air force, which had proved itself already in the Spanish Civil War and Mussolini's Ethiopian campaign in the mid-1930s. The Italians were flying home-produced planes like Capronis and Fiats. Unfortunately for the Italians, their early promise was soon done down by the Desert Air Force.

MALTA ATTACKED

The Regia Aeronautica went into action for the first time on 11 June 1940, with 35 Savoia-Marchetti bombers attacking Malta. Pitted against them were four Gloster Sea Gladiators, constituting the island's only fighter defence force. By the end of the day, the Italians had launched seven attacks for no loss.

By way of response, 26 RAF Bristol Blenheims launched an attack against an Italian airfield in North Africa, eventually destroying 18 enemy aircraft on the ground.

Above: **Despite their years of experience, Italian aircraft and pilots proved no match for the Desert Air Force.**

There followed a number of skirmishes. Prime targets for the Italians were Malta, Gibraltar, the British base at Alexandria in Egypt and the British Mediterranean Fleet.

The action in Africa then forked, with General Graziani leading his contingent of Italians in the Western Desert against Wavell, while the Duke of Aosta led some 215,000 troops out of Italian East Africa and into a British dominion. To meet Graziani's men were the British 7th Armoured Division, soon to be joined by the 6th Australian Division. Meanwhile, the 4th Indian Division was dispatched to meet the threat in East Africa.

It was in the East African campaign that vital steps towards an orchestrated plan for close air support were made. At the outset in October 1940, the Italians in East Africa were a formidable enemy. Their spirits were high, their maturity in desert warfare a major advantage. But much of their buoyancy could be put down to the fact that they enjoyed air superiority. Italy had 14 bomber squadrons or gruppi in East Africa, and five supporting fighter gruppi. The over-stretched British forces, comprising nine squadrons, were happily reinforced by a further eight squadrons from South Africa, flying Hurricane aircraft.

Soon the battle to win supremacy of the skies began to swing in favour of the Allies

Soon, the battle to win supremacy in the skies began to swing in favour of the Allies. Both sides fought bitterly, both on land and in the air, for command of Keren, a fortified hill top in Eritrea. At the end of eight weeks, however, the Italians were turfed out of their stronghold and, by April 1941, a corner in the war of East Africa had been turned. As the campaign toiled on, the South African Air Force formed a first Close Support Flight to co-operate with ground troops, achieving a good measure of success.

FIVE LESSONS

After the battle of Keren, one British observer noted five lessons to be learned. They were: the need for transport planes; the need for supplies to be dropped by air (which was to prove crucial in the jungle wars of Burma and the Pacific); the advantage lent by long-range fighters which could destroy the enemy's aircraft before they lifted off; the need for Red Cross air ambulances to evacuate the wounded; and the preference for dive bombers.

These were all points which would be brought home to subsequent

◆ EYE WITNESS ◆

Ern Stanton, from New South Wales, was 18 when he joined the Royal Australian Air Force and qualified as a flier on the Empire Air Training Scheme.

"Of our EATS course in Canada, about 40 per cent were later killed. It was very sad and disheartening to hear about your mates dying in action but I was really too young and conditioned too much to death to realise the more serious aspects of war

I do particularly remember one little bloke in our squadron who would give away all his personal effects before he went on a mission because he was convinced he wasn't going to come back. When he did return safely, he would go around and get them all back. But he did finally get killed."

senior air force officers. For now, only the immediate achievement of winning an important initial victory was noted. As the Allies took greater command of the action, Italian commanders found themselves battling not only against the Allies but also against a sapped will among their own men. A proportion of their troops were native Africans whose loyalty was suspect.

The campaign in Eritrea was to end in a complete and resounding victory for the Allies by the middle of 1941. Yet short on success though the Allies were at this stage, there was little chance to celebrate. Much as the British commanders had feared, Hitler had sent German forces into the region to assist his floundering fascist soul-mate.

Early in 1941 it was clear the Luftwaffe were installing units of Fliegerkorps X in Sicily, a specialist branch of the air force which had cut its teeth in the Norwegian campaign and specialised in picking off ships. The Mediterranean Fleet first felt its presence on 10 January 1941 when up to 40 aircraft attacked a convoy. In aerial warfare, the Luftwaffe quite simply outclassed the Italians.

At the same time, the conflict in Greece was intensifying. The only assistance actively required by the Greeks at the start was an injection of air power. Here the expanding Allied air strength had little problem asserting its authority. In one battle which took place on 28 February 1941, 16 Hurricanes and 12 Gladiators were patrolling at 14,000 feet when they were attacked by 50

Early in 1941 it was clear that the Luftwaffe were installing units of Fliegerkorps X in Sicily

Below: **Hurricane pilots of 73 Squadron line up before a desert-worn aircraft in North Africa during 1941. The Hurricane was the RAF's first monoplane fighter.**

Above: **German aircraft and pilots suffered the same difficult conditions as their Allied enemies.**

Italian Fiat planes. In the two-hour clash which followed, the Royal Air Force fighters claimed 27 enemy planes for just one Gladiator lost.

The string of successes were a tribute to the ground crews who faced appalling winter conditions in the most primitive of airfields in order to keep the planes airborne. Spring saw further aerial reinforcements sent in by the British but the leaders in the field were uneasy. It was surely only a matter of months before Hitler made that battleground his own as well.

LUFTWAFFE ARRIVES

In April those grim predictions became reality. The Royal Air Force found its forces and those of its Greek and Yugoslav allies suddenly dwarfed by the arrival of the Luftwaffe. Its ranks included 430 bombers, 180 fighters, 700 transport planes and 80 gliders.

By 19 April the four Hurricane squadrons in Greece could rally just 22 operational aircraft between them. All were pulled down to Athens to lend air support to the evacuation of troops from Greece to Crete and North Africa. In the end there were only seven Hurricanes left.

On Crete they were joined by four Sea Gladiators and three Fairey Fulmars of the Fleet Air Arm. The abysmally small fighting force was virtually wiped out on the ground by the marauding Germans.

Added to the boiling pot was the Iraqi uprising against the British in May 1941. The Desert Air Force was by now staffed with Australian, New Zealand, Rhodesian and Free French units, as well as British and South African. But the ceaseless demands took their toll of its strength. And the menace from the Third Reich in the region did nothing to recede during that period. In fact, it gained momentum. Hitler was dallying with the idea of invading Malta. The little island which had found some relief

By 19 April the four Hurricance squadrons in Greece could rally just 22 operational aircraft

when attacking forces were diverted to assist in the invasion of Greece, was once again at the top of the agenda for the Luftwaffe.

MALTA REPLENISHED

Its defences amounted to just four fighter squadrons as well as bombers and Fleet Air Arm forces based off the island. The succession of raids both by the Italians and increasingly by the Germans pared down the number of fighters. But the ranks were replenished on 15 June 1941 when 47 flew from the deck of the Ark Royal, and a further 64 were dispatched by similar means before the month had ended.

The hectic months ahead saw the Malta-based fliers toiling to keep the convoys safe, and so deprive Hitler and Mussolini of the toe-hold they both sought. In addition, they attempted to destroy enemy convoys and hit targets in Italy – particularly Naples where, on 16 December 1941, 16 Wellingtons showered a torpedo factory with 4000lb bombs, the largest used in the Mediterranean to that date.

Between June and October 1941, 220,000 tons of Axis shipping was sunk en route to Libya, of which 115,000 tons could be marked down to the Desert Air Force, especially its Maltese division.

The fruits presented to Churchill by the frustrated Longmore were too few and far between to impress.

On 16 October 1941, 16 Wellingtons showered a Naples torpedo factory with 4,000lb bombs

Friction between the ground and air forces was still very much in evidence, never more so than when a reconnaissance flight reported enemy troops approaching a vital petrol dump in

Below: **SS *Talbot* was one of scores of ships to fall foul of enemy planes in Malta's Grand Harbour.**

◆ EYE WITNESS ◆

Post Office worker Arthur Helm was one of the first New Zealanders to sign up and fight for Britain following the outbreak of World War II.

"I had read a lot about the Germans and I knew how despicable they were. And I knew what I was letting myself in for.

I was a member of the First Echelon, the 6,607 men who first left New Zealand for Eygpt. Later I was in northern Greece as a member of 4th Brigade Signals. After the invasion of the Germans, we moved to fight a rearguard action at Thebes. I saw the Acropolis about four hours before the Swastika was raised over it. At Port Rafti we held a two-mile stretch of coastline and two miles inland during the evacuation. We had to throw everything overboard except for our rifles, the clothes we stood up in and a small haversack.

Author Laurence Durrell wrote that when everyone arrived in Crete they were dishevelled, dispirited and defeated – except the New Zealanders. They came up the beach with their rifles poised, their hats on and every one had a book under his arms. He was wrong – I had two books, a book of poetry and a Bible.

Spirits were high among the New Zealanders. We simply felt sorry for the Greek soldiers we left behind.

We expected the arrival of the Germans. I had just knocked off after 24 hours on duty and was having my breakfast when the first parachutes appeared.

There was a lot of deer-stalking and rabbit-shooting in New Zealand so most of us could shoot pretty straight. You knew when you had hit a parachutist coming down. He retracted his legs up as an automatic reaction.

Later I got involved at Galatas where we went in with bayonets after dark and drove out a bunch of Germans from the houses there. It was very nerve-racking but we got rid of them – even if we did have to retreat the next day.

I got out over the mountains to the harbour for evacuation. I met an English soldier at the side of the track and pointed out the way. He said: "I'm not going any further." I gave him some water and he told me he had been through Dunkirk but it wasn't a patch on this.

He just laid down on the hillside and died. He was done for, absolutely exhausted, and he had no will to live.

We lost Crete because the Germans had planes and we didn't. But we never lost heart. After being evacuated from Crete we went to Sidi Rezburgh. That was probably the worst campaign of the lot."

***Above:* On Malta, air strips like this one provided constant targets for Luftwaffe pilots. *Right:* Air Chief Marshal Sir Arthur Tedder.**

the North African desert. The dump was destroyed before it was discovered the troops in question were, in fact, British. Never mind that it was notoriously difficult to positively identify the nationality of soldiers from the air. The fighters on the ground had been deprived of valuable fuel for no reason. Longmore's repeated requests for more aircraft did little to endear him at home, either. Duly, Longmore was replaced by Arthur Tedder in May 1941.

AIR FLEET ENLARGED

The following month, Wavell was dispatched from North Africa by an irate Churchill. Happily, his replacement, General Sir Claude Auchinleck, struck an immediate harmonious note with Tedder which helped to end the bubbling army-air force discord.

Tedder, with support from the Air Ministry, helped to overhaul the repair and maintenance operations in the region which were proving so inefficient and therefore costly to the service.

Once he had enlarged the fleet of aircraft available to the Desert Air Force to beyond 1,000 in November 1941, Tedder turned his attention to the quest for new, well-trained recruits. There was a chronic shortage of training facilities in the Middle East.

Two operations to relieve Tobruk, 'Brevity' and "Battleaxe', had failed in the early summer of 1941

Tedder fell back on his usual standpoint, which was to employ an expert – in this case Air Commodore B. Embry – who could devote the best of his time and attention to the problem.

CO-ORDINATED ACTION

Two operations to relieve Tobruk, 'Brevity' and 'Battleaxe', had failed in the early summer of 1941 and once again it seemed the relations between army and air force would be strained. It was in September 1941 that a satisfactory blueprint for co-ordinated action was finally drawn up to at last eliminate this problem. Drawing on the illustrations of the East African campaign, it set out the principles of close support of land forces by air forces, including pre-arranged and impromptu attacks on the enemy. Indirect air support was defined as attacks on objectives other than the enemy forces in the battle proper.

Above: **Air Chief Marshal Sir Arthur W. Tedder, Deputy Supreme Commander, Allied Forces Western Europe.**

An Air Support Control headquarters was created for each army corps. These were information exchanges linked by two-way radio to brigades in action. Representing the RAF at brigade was a team called a Forward Air Support Link. The RAF team could assess the action at close quarters and request air support when necessary. On receiving the request, the staff at the Air Support Control team headquarters, with its overview, could work out where best to send its aircraft during a battle for the most effective results.

The principles had already been put into practice on exercises in Northern Ireland as early as September 1940. A developmental Army Co-Operation Command had been set up by the RAF following Dunkirk when the air force received flak for not coming more visibly to the aid of evacuating soldiers.

In Africa, these close-support principles were not only rehearsed but put into action as well, and adopted thereafter to the satisfaction of everyone involved.

THE END OF THE BEGINNING..

'This is not the end. It is not even the beginning of the end. But it is, perhaps, the end of the beginning.'

(Winston Churchill after the Allied victory in North Africa.)

REDS IN THE SKY

No one in Russia was ready for war when it came in June 1941, least of all the unwieldy air force.

Stalin boasted of a large body of planes. But like the sizeable French air force of 1940, the Red Air Force was ineffectively used and no match for the skill and experience of the Luftwaffe. Its sole four-engined bomber at the outset of the war was the TB-3, slow, underpowered and inadequately armed. It had ten squadrons of MiG, Yak and Lagg fighters. Yet these were far inferior to the Messerschmitts so elegantly handled by German pilots.

Above: Britain provided Hurricanes and know-how to the Russian air force, following the German invasion.

In addition, the Russians were partway through a modernisation plan in which their outdated planes would be replaced by more competitive models. The Russian air force, like all branches of the establishment, had suffered its fair share of losses in the purges which Stalin organised to rid himself of potential opponents.

AID FROM BRITAIN

The pilots of the Red Air Force were trained to support the troops on the ground rather than enter into combat with other aircraft. Many ended up frantically helping to evacuate Russian industry to the east, to save it from falling into German hands – reducing the aircraft available for other duties still further. Indeed, its fighter arm had never been put to the test. The summer and autumn of 1941 brought a succession of disasters for the Red Air Force.

Still being punished by the Germans at home, the RAF nevertheless found the resources to send several squadrons of Hurricanes to the aid of the Russians.

It was Churchill's wish that as much aid should be devoted to the beleaguered and reluctant new ally as possible – despite the fact he was a lifelong critic of communism. In a broadcast shortly after Hitler's 'Operation Barbarossa', he explained how the hatred of fascism remained uppermost in his emotions.

The summer and autumn of 1941 brought a succession of disasters for the Red Air Force

Left: Much of Russia's air power was devoted to shipping industry east.
Far left: The TB-7 bomber that brought Russian minister Molotov to Britain.

'The Nazi regime is indistinguishable from the worst features of Communism. It is devoid of all theme and principle except appetite and racial domination. It excels all forms of human wickedness in the efficiency of its cruelty and ferocious aggression. No one has been a more consistent opponent of Communism that I have for the last 25 years. I will unsay no word that I have spoken about it.

BRITISH TEACHERS

'But all this fades away before the spectacle which is now unfolding. The past, with its crimes, its follies and its tragedies, flashes away. I see the Russian soldiers standing on the threshold of their native land, guarding the fields which their fathers have tilled from time immemorial. I see them guarding their homes where mothers and wives pray . . .

'I see the Russian soldiers standing on the threshold of their native land'

'I see advancing upon all this in hideous onslaught the Nazi war machine with its clanking, heel-clicking, dandified Prussian officers, its crafty expert agents fresh from the cowing and tying down of a dozen countries . . .

'I see the German bombers and fighters in the sky, still smarting from many a British whipping, delighted to find what they believe is an easier and safer prey.

'. . . if Hitler imagines that his attack on Soviet Russia will cause the slightest divergence of aims or slackening of effort in the great democracies who are resolved upon his doom, he is woefully mistaken.'

A British unit was sent with the aircraft to the Soviet Union to teach the Russians how to make and fly Hurricanes and to oass on tactical tips about the escort of bombers and general air operations.

Below: **Royal Air Force Hurricanes pictured in the air over the Russian countryside on their way back to base from escort duty.**

◆ EYE WITNESS ◆

Alexander Pokryshkin, the son of a bricklayer in Novosibirsk in Siberia, emerged as one of Russia's air aces. He flew 550 operational flights, fought 137 aerial battles and had 59 victories to his credit. He became the first member of the Soviet armed forces to be awarded the title 'Hero of the Soviet Union' three times, receiving his third Hero's Gold Star Medal in August 1944.

❛ I was out with pilot Semyonov as my partner flying on a reconnaissance mission to Jassy where the Germans had an aerodrome. As we approached the town I espied five Messerschmitts flying towards us, three below us and two above. Here, at last, were live Germans. They spotted us. I rocked my wings as a signal to Semyonov that I was going to attack. There were five of them and only two of us.

I was flying a MiG-3. It is a sturdy machine and well armed. It behaves wonderfully at high altitudes when its speed and manoeuvrability increase. I had my plan of action all worked out in an instant. Semyonov was to cover me as we had previously arranged on the ground. I shot up into the clouds and kept on climbing until I ran into one of the two Messerschmitts coming towards me. The German zoomed almost in my face. I did a stall-turn and found myself on the tail of the yellow, blunt-winged craft. I fired at short range. The Messerschmitt burst into flames and plunged downwards. I watched it as it fell and that almost cost me my life. The other German had crept up behind me. White ribbons of his tracers shot by and then my plane shuddered. Its port wing had been torn by bullets.

I dived to zero feet and hedge-hopped all the way home and, feeling that my aircraft was losing stability all the time, with great difficulty got back to the airfield. I made a normal landing, taxied to a stop, shut off the engine and slumped aganst the armoured back of the seat. I needed a drink. My throat was parched. That was the first German I had bagged. ❜

Soon, the lessons of the visiting Britons and that of bitter experience began to sink in. Until the Russians became fully conversant with combat know-how and were better equipped, however, a handful of German pilots had a field day.

King of the skies at that time was Erich Hartmann, otherwise known as 'Bubi' Hartmann or the 'Blond Knight'. During World War II he scored a record 352 victories, or kills, all of which were validated, making him an 'ace of aces'. Most were made on the Eastern front.

Hartmann was born in Weissach, near Stuttgart, on 19 April 1922. As a boy, he lived in China where his father was a doctor. When the family returned to Germany Hartmann was encouraged by his mother, herself a pilot, to sample the joys of flight. First qualifying as a glider pilot and instructor, Hartmann then joined the Luftwaffe aged 18.

He revealed the secret of his success: 'My only tactics are to wait until I have the chance to attack the enemy then close in at high speed. I open fire only when the whole windshield is black with the enemy. Then not a single shot goes wild. I hit the enemy with all my guns and he goes down.'

During World War II Hartmann scored a record 352 kills, all of which were validated

In his beloved Me-109, he knocked out seven Red Air Force planes above the Battle of Kursk on 7 July 1943. It wasn't unusual for him to return from a sortie with more than one kill to his credit. No Allied pilot even approached such a mighty score.

HARTMANN ESCAPES

Operating over Russia, his plane was once shot down. Although he was unhurt, he was taken prisoner by Russian soldiers – a fate dreaded by German airmen at the time.

He pretended he was injured and was placed on a stretcher in a truck. En route to find a doctor he sprang up, overpowered his guard and leapt under fire from the lorry into a field of sunflowers. Sleeping by day and walking by night, he finally reached the German lines where he was almost shot by one of the sentries.

His outstanding success and distinctly Ayran features made him a

Above: **Russian pilots are congratulated by their major after completing a mission on the Eastern front.**

Below: **Erich Hartmann was one of the most successful pilots of the war, scoring most of his victories over Russia.**

favourite with Adolf Hitler who awarded him the Knight's Cross and later added the prestigious German military decorations of Oak Leaves, Swords and, finally, Diamonds. Courageous not only in the air, he frequently had cross words with his German superiors. Once he was even drunk enough to begin juggling with the Führer's hat but still remained a 'golden boy'.

■ HARD LABOUR ■

Erich Hartmann scored his last victory on the final day of the war, having flown 1,400 missions. He then came down to earth with a jolt, being captured by Russians. His sentence following the war was 25 years' hard labour – although he was offered freedom if he agreed to settle in East Germany and train their air force. He refused the deal and was finally released in 1956 following negotiations by Chancellor Adenauer of West Germany.

Hartmann resumed his air force career and learned to fly jets under

ACE PILOTS

In the league table of wartime ace pilots, the first five places are occupied by Germans followed by two Japanese and a Finnish pilot. The first pilot from the West to appear in the league comes in 27th place, South African J. Pattle, who is followed by Richard Bong (below) and Thomas McGuire of the US and J. Johnson of Britain.

the auspices of the Americans. He was married in 1944 to his wartime sweetheart Ursula Puetsch, and the couple had a daughter. Hartmann died in 1993, aged 71.

As 1941 closed, the prospects improved considerably for the Russians in the air war. The Luftwaffe having deployed the majority of its air power in the opening stages of 'Operation Barbarossa', its strength on the Eastern front soon waned as it became overstretched and struggled to maintain its operations on three fronts.

LUFTWAFFE SUFFERS

Worse was to come for the German air forces remaining on the Eastern front. Luftwaffe field divisions were created to back up the ground forces as the conflict with Russia dragged on, and a final total of 200,000 men abandoned their air duties to become infantrymen. It left the air crews short of ground staff. They were also to suffer from lack of aircraft and fuel and a diminishing training programme.

Worse was to come for the German air forces remaining on the Eastern front

Russian industry which had moved to the safety of the east was able to produce supplies for the Red Air Force – which was further bolstered by American aircraft through the Lend-Lease Act.

Below: **With much of Russia's powerful industrial muscle in the safety of the east, Stalin was able to provide his air force with vital replacement planes and components when Hitler could not.**

TIGER, TIGER, TIGER

By 1941, tensions were running high between the Americans and Japan. The United States government looked on uncomfortably as Japan sought to expand its empire by waging a brutal war on China.

Although Japan's leaders pledged neutrality in the European war, alarm bells were sounding across the Western world. Both America and its future allies aided the hard-pressed Chinese.

Seizing a golden opportunity in September 1940, the Japanese pushed the boundaries of their empire back by moving into Indochina at the expense of Vichy France, the colonial rulers of the country. This was a move the European puppet state was powerless to resist. In retaliation the anxious and angry United States and Britain broke off trading relations, which meant a halt to the supply of vital oil to Japan. The exiled Dutch government did likewise. Australia was by now viewing the aspirations of Japan with trepidation.

Without oil, Japan could survive for 18 months at the most despite the huge stockpiles it had imported during the 1930s. At stake was its considerable economic might. The hawks among the Japanese hierarchy quickly argued that time was running out for Japan and that a military strike to consolidate its position was needed sooner rather than later.

TRIPARTITE PACT

In the same month as the threatening manoeuvres in Indochina, Japan joined with aggressors Germany and Italy in the Tripartite Pact, which set out a code of co-operation between the three. There could be little doubt now that the Land of the Rising Sun was poised on the brink of war. But the question which troubled the Americans was, just how would the inevitable conflict begin?

Japan had sound reasoning behind the desire to enlarge its lands. In 1939, its population reached 99 million and was increasing at the rate of five million a year. Its home islands were becoming overcrowded and overstretched. Britain, France and Holland all enjoyed the benefits of colonies. America, although ideologically opposed to colonialism,

In September 1940 Japan joined with aggressors Germany and Italy in the Tripartite Pact

Left: **An aerial view of the US Pacific Fleet's base at Pearl Harbor.**
Below: **Japan's foreign minister Matsuoka talks with Ribbentrop in early 1941.**

had its spheres of influence. Japan felt entitled to the same. It was not unreasonable, the Japanese felt, for their country to hold sway over the Pacific and China.

Japan's transformation from feudal backwater to burgeoning world power had been rapid. It was only in the latter half of the 19th century that Japan had come out of isolation. After that, the Japanese followed the

The Japanese felt cheated, unable to trust the countries they had known as friends

British and American examples and were set on a programme of industrialisation. Yet the new breed of manufacturers struggled to compete on the same terms as the Westerners. Britain had tariffs which discouraged overseas trade while America also followed a policy of protectionism.

Nevertheless, Japan joined the Allies during World War I. After-

Right: **Japanese pilots were hailed as heroes back home after their unannounced attack on the US Pacific Fleet's base at Pearl Harbor.**

wards, the Japanese were anxious to be accepted as part of the New World Order on equal terms with other nations. Bitter disappointment was in store.

At the Paris peace conference the Japanese proposed a clause of racial equality, with the aim of ironing out the discrimination they had previously felt, once and for all. The emissaries from Japan assumed that there would be no controversy over the clause's acceptance.

JAPANESE ANGER

In the event, it was barred by none other than American president Woodrow Wilson, who went on to place a ban on Japanese people entering the US when immigration by other nationalities was rife. Australia, too, had a 'whites only' immigration policy. The Japanese felt cheated and angry, unable to trust the countries they had hitherto known as friends. Western powers seemed more fraudulent than ever when the Washington Treaty of 1922 was drawn up, limiting Japan to just three capital ships for every five run by both the US and Britain.

The Japanese largely followed Western models of democracy. Although there was an emperor, he was bound by the decisions of his ministers. Yet the Japanese government differed sharply from others in one vital respect. Its civilian ministers ran civil affairs. But there were ministers from the army and navy entirely responsible for military matters. Without the co-operation of those ministers from the armed services, the government fell. It meant they wielded huge power. To further complicate matters, there was an enormous degree of rivalry between the army and the navy and the two services could rarely agree.

Aside from these wranglings, there was also the sinister threat of assassination. It became a political tool increasingly used among young patriots. Those in power became cautious, corrupt and sly. There came a feeling among the Japanese that politicians

Left: **Admiral Isoroku Yamamoto was the architect of the strike against Pearl Harbor. Yet he feared he had 'awakened a sleeping giant'.**

PEARL HARBOR

On the morning of 7 December 1941, the Japanese attacked on Pearl Harbor. As the US naval base prepared for its day, Japanese carrier aircraft swept in and tore into the US Pacific Fleet at rest. The fleet's carriers were at sea, but the battleships were in. *Arizona, West Virginia, California* and *Oklahoma* were destroyed; *Pennsylvania, Nevada, Tennessee* and *Maryland* were damaged. The Japanese lost nine Zeroes, 15 'Vals' and five 'Kates'.

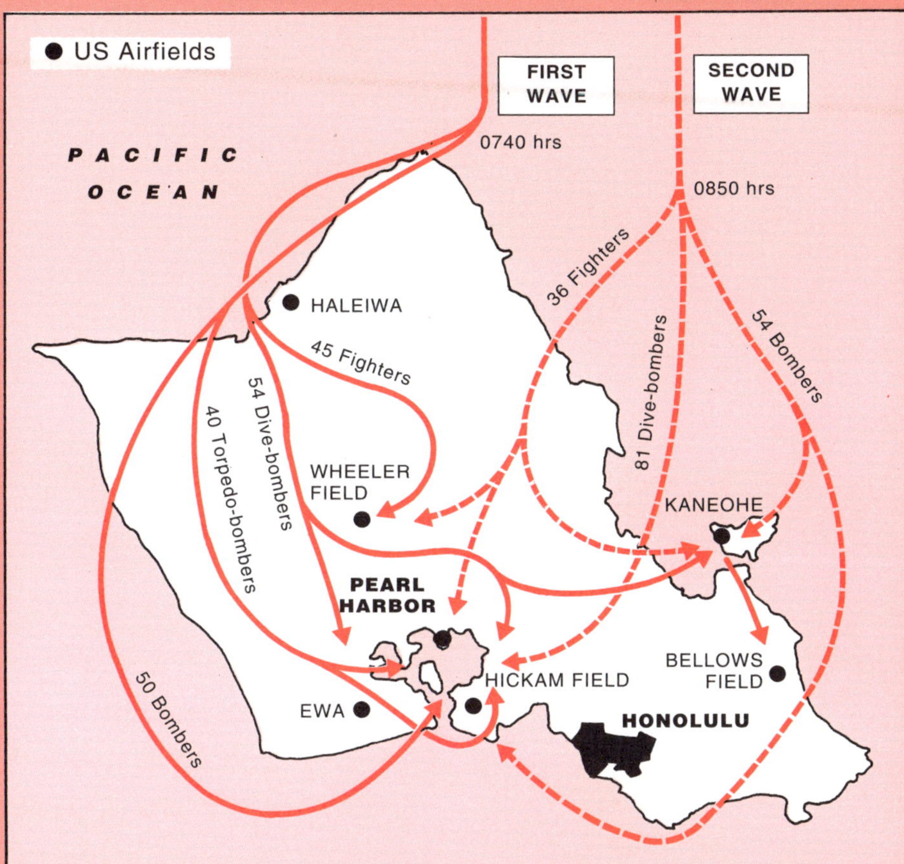

could not be trusted. Not only that, there was widespread fear about the encroachment of communism. Together with a growing admiration for the achievements of Nazi Germany, Japan swung towards militarism.

Japan, still cut out from overseas trade by the policies adopted by key trading partners Britain and America, began to feel the pinch during the Great Depression of the 1930s. Japan spent much of the 1930s meddling in internal Chinese affairs. When China became unwilling and belligerent, the two countries finally went to war. In 1937, Japan withdrew from the League of Nations and denounced the Washington Treaty, privately planning to increase its naval strength to compare with that of Britain. And she sought to boost her empire.

YAMAMOTO'S PLAN

Casting greedy eyes at the colonies in South East Asia and the Pacific owned by Britain, Holland and France, Japanese military leaders realised the outposts were now vulnerable, with the mother countries being embroiled in problems thousands of miles away. The remote islands were economically wealthy, precisely why they were incorporated into empires in the first place. Japan would become stronger than ever before if only it could avail itself of the assets there.

With Japan's vast military might, the islands were easy enough targets. But the Japanese leadership rightly guessed that America was unlikely to sit back and watch as it established a thriving Pacific or Asiatic powerbase. It would, of course, send its big ships to trouble-spots. The answer, it seemed, was to knock out the mighty American navy to obtain the necessary freedom of the seas.

The answer, it seemed, was to knock out the mighty American navy

Conveniently, the pride of the US fleet was based in Hawaii, much closer to Japan than the inaccessible mainland of the United States. And so the infamous attack on Pearl Harbor was conceived.

It was a brilliant short-term strategy drawn up by Admiral Yamamoto. Key to its success was the element of surprise. There was a hard summer of training for the pilots of the fighters, dive-bombers and torpedo-bombers which were to be shipped in for the pre-emptive strike. Most Japanese pilots had seen plenty of action in the war with China.

To ensure the action, code-named 'Operation Z', was effective, powerful six-inch naval shells were adapted for use by the aircraft, sufficient to plough through the armour of US battleships. The Japanese also had a 24-inch torpedo known as the 'Long

Right: **Japanese aircraft warm up on the deck of the carrier Hiryu before delivering their stunning blow to the US Navy at Pearl Harbor.**

Lance', containing 1,000 pounds of explosives; it was among the most powerful weapons in the world.

As early as 26 November 1941 the Japanese navy set off from its base, using an obscure route and maintaining complete radio silence. By 7 December it was in position, 270 miles north of Pearl Harbor in the Kurile Islands.

'TIGER, TIGER, TIGER'

The fleet, under Vice-Admiral Chuiki Nagumo, comprised six aircraft carriers, with a capacity of 423 planes. In the attack 360 were used, the force comprising 104 high-level bombers, 135 dive-bombers, 40 torpedo-bombers and 81 fighters. In addition, the escort force consisted of two battleships, three cruisers, submarines and supply ships.

In dock at Pearl Harbor were 96 American ships. Fortunately for the US, the base's two aircraft carriers were at sea. Their destruction may have altered the course of the war.

At Pearl Harbor, a new day was beginning, clouded only by a general fear of war. Still, the beaches were silvery, the sun was warm and the majority of the servicemen based there were looking forward to a day of relaxation. Many were still in bed when the storm broke.

Although America had been forewarned that Japan was planning a major strike, it didn't know where or when it would take place. Most thought the Philippines the obvious target for Japanese aggression. The ships in Pearl Harbor were undefended, their ammunition safely held in lockers.

The only clue to the carnage to come came in the early hours when a periscope was spotted in the harbour

The ships in Pearl Harbor were undefended, their ammunition in lockers

Left: **Pearl Harbor explodes under the onslaught of Japanese bombs. Fortunately, key fuel installations were left intact, so averting utter disaster.**

PEARL HARBOR

US Losses
18 ships, including 8 battleships, sunk or badly damaged; 164 aircraft destroyed and 124 aircraft damaged; 2,403 men dead and 1,178 men wounded.

Japanese Losses
29 aircraft downed; 5 midget submarines sunk; 64 men dead or missing; 1 prisoner taken.

mouth. A destroyer duly went out to sink the unidentified submarine.

In fact, few people outside the navy top brass in Tokyo knew what was going on. Unwilling to announce its intentions and give its game away, Japan didn't deliver its declaration of war to America until Pearl Harbor was smoking.

At 6am the first wave of aircraft took off and headed for Hawaii. As they came in sight of Pearl Harbor Captain Mitsuo Fuchida, in command of the first wave, broadcast to his men, screaming 'Tora, Tora, Tora' – 'Tiger, Tiger, Tiger', literally translated. The message informed them that the Americans were still unaware of what was to come. At 7.56am the first shots rang out. In neat formations, the skilful, well-practised pilots made runs over the lines of vessels anchored along 'Battleship Row', the section of the harbour where the capital ships lay.

As they came in sight, Fuchida broadcast to his men, screaming 'Tora, Tora, Tora'

Below: **US servicemen at Pearl Harbor were staggered at the sight that greeted them. Japanese aggression was dubbed 'treachery' around the Allied world.**

Far below them, braving the telltale shallow waters of the harbour, were Japanese midget submarines, each one hoping to bag a battleship.

A stunned commander ordered them to take action, bellowing 'This is no drill!'

Ship after ship was blasted and soon the air was filled with thick, spiralling, oily black plumes of smoke. As the flaming oil from one stricken vessel spilled into the sea, it set light to another. The second wave of Japanese bombers had difficulty locating targets through the fug.

The Arizona was hit and exploded – 1,200 members of her crew died. The battleships West Virginia, Oklahoma, and California were also destroyed, and Nevada, Maryland, Tennessee, and Pennsylvania were damaged. Further casualties included the cruisers Honolulu, Raleigh and St Helena, and the destroyers Shaw, Cassin and Downs. These ships, all symbols of America's greatness, were left tattered wrecks.

In the midst of the chaos a contingent of American aircraft arrived. Their pilots must have gaped in disbelief at the scenes before them. What once was a landing strip had been set ablaze, along with most of the aircraft on it. Then they too were attacked, no match for the nimble Japanese fliers. The same fate was in store for the crews of dive-bombers from the absent carrier Enterprise who returned to base during the attack.

29 PLANES DOWNED

At times the Japanese pilots screeched in so low they were clearly visible to the frantic Americans.

The men at Pearl Harbor responded to the onslaught with considerable zest. A stunned commander ordered them to take action, bellowing the words: 'This is no drill!' Despite the shock and disbelief, the Americans soon manned the guns as they had done before in training and claimed 29

Below: **'Battleship Row' at Pearl Harbor provided rich pickings for the carrier-borne aircraft of Yamamoto's strike force.**

Above: **Despite the suddenness of the strike, troops rushed to man the guns. A total of 29 Japanese planes – nine Zeroes, 15 'Vals' and five 'Kates' were downed.**

Japanese planes. Others raced to rescue comrades trapped in blazing ships or operated firefighting equipment. Finally, there was calm. The surviving servicemen set about their grim tasks with one ear open for the return of the Japanese.

While the Pacific Fleet's base was extensively damaged, it was not crippled, since the fuelling and repair depots had escaped unscathed. It was to take months, however, and in some cases years, to refloat and repair the shattered bodywork of the damaged ships.

The Japanese did not return to finish off the base, as was widely feared among US servicemen and their families. Well satisfied with the results of the operation, which went better than any of the Japanese commanders dared hope, Vice-Admiral Nagumo decided a quick, getaway was now in order, particularly as fuel was running dangerously low, and the US carriers Lexington and Enterprise might appear.

In America there was outrage and horror at the loss of life. US secretary of state Cordell Hull was still in conference with Japanese negotiators when news of the attack reached him. They had already presented him with a document purporting to set out the area of debate.

A REPEAT OF 1904

Mr Hull furiously declared: 'In all my 50 years of public service I have never seen a document that was more crowded with infamous falsehoods and distortions on a scale so huge that I never imagined until today that any government on this planet was capable of uttering them.'

Although some took the opportunity to condemn President Franklin Roosevelt for his lack of readiness, most American citizens were determined to pull behind him in their fury at the Japanese action.

Ironically, the attack on Pearl Harbor mirrored a military move made by the Japanese against the Russians in 1904. Once again, without an official declaration of war, the Japanese navy carried out a surprise attack on a key Russian base, picking off some prestige targets. Back then, The Times of London hailed it as 'an act of daring' and praised the Japanese for their initiative and vigour.

In Britain, the Daily Mail now voiced the venom of many when it wrote: 'Not even Hitler has yet achieved the infamy of a stab in the back while his envoys were still ostensibly negotiating terms of agreement with his intended victim.

'This is an act which the world will never forget so long as the records of history are read. It will stand for all time as an example of the ultimate depths of deceit to which it is possible for any nation to descend.'

> ***On 8 December, both America and Britain officially declared war on Japan***

On 8 December, both America and Britain officially declared war on Japan. In response to the declaration and the wave of Japanese attacks around the region, the Royal Navy battleship Prince of Wales and battlecruiser Repulse sailed out of Singapore with an escort of four destroyers. Disastrously, 'Force Z', as it was known, ignored the threat of airborne action and left without the protection of an aircraft carrier. Their aim was to prevent the Japanese making landings on British-held territory in South East Asia. But the mission went badly wrong when the

◆ EYE WITNESS ◆

Kazuo Sakamaki was the commander of a midget submarine, one of five which was sent into action at Pearl Harbor.

Something went wrong. At the moment of release my submarine nearly toppled over into the water. The trim had not worked well. I feared that if we attempted to emerge hastily enemy observers might spot the ship. I remembered that the opening of hostilities was to follow the handing of the notice of war to the US government. If by my own mistake the presence of the Japanese forces should be discovered it would create a grave problem. It would spoil the air attack and every other detail of the carefully worked-out plan. I could not cause such a blunder. No matter how dangerous the condition of my ship I could not let it emerge to the surface.

My aide and I crawled back and forth inside the submarine removing the lead ballast and filling the tanks with water to correct the trim of the craft. It had been our plan that by midnight all five submarines would be inside the harbour and would sink to the bottom and wait for the dawn. But when I looked at the watch it was midnight already. The ship righted itself.

I figured that as long as we entered the harbour during the night no damage would have been done. I drank a bit of wine and ate my lunch.

"Let's do our utmost." My comrade and I held each other's hands and pledged success. I took my position and moved forward with minimum speed.

After ten minutes I lifted the ship slightly to see through the telescope where we were going. To my horror, the ship was moving in the wrong direction.

Moving blindly because my gyrocompass was not working, the ship had gone 90 degrees off her course. If I could manage the ship with the help of the telescope we could get back on our course but this was clearly impossible.

"We must get to the mouth of the harbour" I repeated to myself. My hands were wet with cold sweat. I changed the direction three or four times, hoping against hope that somehow the ship would get going where I wanted to go. The speed was maintained at the minimum as before.

Time ticked away in complete indifference to my predicament. It was almost the moment for attack.

As we came nearer to the enemy ships guarding the entrance I was able to see the white uniforms of the sailors aboard. I concluded they were destroyers.

I pushed the midget submarine toward them, Suddenly I heard an enormous noise and felt the ship shaking. I was hit on the head and lost consciousness. This was my first contact with war.

I came to myself in a short while and saw white smoke in my submarine. I changed the speed to half gear and turned the ship around. I wanted to see if any damage had been done. My comrade was all right. My two torpedoes were all right. I did not want to waste my torpedoes on those destroyers which began again to charge against me. They threw depth charges at us. They fell near us but not as close as the first time.

two British giants became sitting ducks for the Japanese Naval Air Arm flying out of Indochina.

The Prince of Wales, able to fire 60,000 shells every minute out of its array of 175 anti-aircraft guns, was thought to be impregnable. The cream of Japan's pilots didn't think so.

On 10 December, both ships were sunk off the coast of Malaya within an hour of each other and 800 members of their crews were killed, although 2,000 were saved by the accompanying destroyers. Among the dead was the leader of the ill-fated squadron, Admiral Tom Spencer Vaughan Phillips. There were 34 high-level bombers and 51 torpedo-bombers coming at the ships from all directions. Only three aircraft had to be ditched. The formidable Japanese fliers had struck again. Winston Churchill heard the news by telephone from the Chief of Naval Staff. 'I never received a more direct shock,' he commented.

As militarily admirable as it might have seemed to the Japanese at the time, the long-term consequences of the attack on Pearl Harbor were clearly ill thought-out. Japan had a

Left: **Both Roosevelt and Cordell Hull were disgusted by the Japanese attack.**

magnificent navy, powerful enough to compete with that of America or Britain, with the most modern aircraft carrier fleet in the world. Its army too was large and capable.

A GIANT AWAKENED

Yet Japan could not have possibly hoped to complete its victory with an occupation of the US. It was a geographical and numerical impossibility. And if the leaders of Japan hoped the action at Pearl Harbor would demoralise the Americans and encourage them to capitulate, they sorely misjudged their foe. The aim seems to have been merely to cause enough damage to keep America at bay while Japan built up its strength in the Pacific.

It is likely they were then hoping for a war of attrition in which America would weary and compromise. Yet architect of the deadly war strike Admiral Yamamoto clearly had an inclination of what lay ahead when he said: 'I fear we have only awakened a sleeping giant and his reaction will be terrible.'

Nervy? Then you need SANATOGEN Nerve-Tonic Food

Daily Mail

LATE WAR NEWS SPECIAL

BLACK & WHITE It's the Scotch

NO. 14,233 ONE PENNY FOR KING AND EMPIRE MONDAY, DECEMBER 8, 1941

JAPAN DECLARES WAR ON BRITAIN AND AMERICA

Heavy Bombing of Honolulu and Guam: Hundreds Dead

'BRITISH WARSHIPS IN ACTION' REPORT

From DON IDDON New York, Sunday.

JAPAN to-night declared war on Britain and the United States after launching full-scale naval and air attacks on two of America's main bases in the Pacific—Pearl Harbour, in Hawaii, and Guam, between Hawaii and the Philippine Islands. Already the Dutch East Indies have announced themselves at war with Japan, and the formal British and American declarations are expected in a matter of hours.

Quickly recovering from the first attacks, American warships steamed out of Pearl Harbour, and it was later reported that a Japanese aircraft-carrier had been sunk. Four Japanese submarines and six aircraft are also said to have been destroyed.

The Columbia Broadcasting System claims to have picked up a message saying that two British cruisers were sunk by Japanese planes attacking Singapore. This report is completely without confirmation.

Another message, equally without support but well within the bounds of possibility, is that Japanese warships have been engaged by British and American naval units in the Western Pacific.

This report emanates from the Tokio correspondent of a Japanese newspaper in Shanghai quoting an announcement by Imperial Headquarters.

Early reports that Manila, the American base in the Philippine Islands, had been raided

PARLIAMENT TO-DAY

BOTH Houses of Parliament will meet at 3 p.m. to-day, it was officially announced from Downing-street last night. A statement will be made in the Lords and Commons.

Mr. Churchill will give M.P.s a full review of the situation arising from Japan's latest aggression, it is understood.

Japanese Seize Shanghai

British Gunboat Sunk by Shells

From Daily Mail Correspondent

Shanghai, Sunday.

JAPANESE forces to-day took over the Shanghai International Settlement

New York All Set for Air Raids

From WALTER FARR Washington, Sunday

MAYOR LAGUARDIA, of New York, called his Civil Defence chiefs to a conference to-night to take every precaution against possible air raids on the city. The Fire Department sent out a warning to all firemen.

So far there is no black-out, but the Fire Commissioner said the department was prepared to institute one to-night if necessary.

The mayor said the Japanese activities were "master-minded" by the thugs and gangsters who control

EMBASSY IS 'WIDE OPEN'

DESERT BATTLE RAGES

STRONG British forces, on land and in the air, were attacking yesterday the 21st and 15th German armoured divisions which had been moving to the west.

Attacks were also launched on masses of enemy transport, spread out apparently in disorder along miles of road.

Mobile British columns are swiftly mopping up scattered groups of Germans and Italians in the Sidi Rezegh area cut off from their supplies.

Tobruk Tank Battle—BACK Page.

Bombs Fall on East Coast

Incendiary and high-explosive bombs were dropped by a single raider last night on an east coast town. There were several minor casualties and a few small fires which were quickly put out.

LATEST

CANADA DECLARES WAR ON JAPAN

Canada declared war on Japan this morning.

Reported that general mobilisation has been ordered in Dutch East Indies. R.A.F. have been invited to station planes in the Indies.

The tiny Central American republic of Costa Rica has declared war on Japan, and the Cuban Parliament has been summoned.—A.P. messages.

Above: **British newspapers joined the wave of indignation against the war-mongering Japanese after their opening strikes in the Pacific.**

◆ EYE WITNESS ◆

A correspondent for the National Broadcasting Corporation gave this account of the bombing of Pearl Harbor.

'The most thickly populated air base was attacked by Japanese planes a little after 8 am local time.

After machine-gunning Ford Island the Japanese planes moved to Hickman Field. Observers say that considerable damage was done there but a number of planes were brought down.

Three ships of the United States Pacific Fleet based at Pearl Harbor were attacked and the 29,000-ton battleship *Oklahoma* was set on fire.

All lines of communication appear to be down between the various Army and Navy aerodromes and the Army in the field.

The Army has issued orders for all people to remain off the streets.

The first raiders carried torpedoes and did considerable damage to shipping in Pearl Harbor and off Honolulu. They came in squadron formation over Diamond Head, dropping high explosives and incendiary bombs.

They came over Honolulu itself and were at once met with anti-aircraft from Pearl Harbor, Ford Island, Wheeler Field, Honolulu Municipal Airport, Hickman Field and the new Navy repair base.

A terrific barrage was put up but all the points I mentioned appear to have been attacked.

The chief of fire services has reported that the fires were under control and were not as bad as expected.'

AERIAL WEAPONRY

Ripe for exploitation, bursting with potential, the aeroplane came of age during World War II. It could never win battles alone. But the aircraft of those troubled years undeniably made the difference between triumph and wholesale military failure. While they would never replace ground troops, they did succeed in making giant battleships obsolete and changed the face of modern conflict.

Incredibly, following World War I, British politicians, including eminent figures like Prime Minister Stanley Baldwin, were all for scrapping military 'wings'. French marshal Ferdinand Foch summed up the prevailing attitude when he said: 'Aviation is good sport but for the army it is useless.'

It was only the vociferous campaigning of Lord Hugh Trenchard, Marshal of the Royal Air Force during the 1920s, that kept the RAF in business. It was the same story across the Atlantic where sceptics failed to see a future in flight. William Mitchell, assistant chief of the US Army Air Service, faced similar negative reactions against the budding force. He managed to silence some of the critics with trial bombardments between 1921 and 1923 which sank six warships. Still, jealousies levied in America by the existing well-established branches of the military mirrored those in Britain.

SHANGHAI BLITZ

These were people who failed to read the writing on the wall. German air attacks by Zeppelins and aircraft in south east England during World War I claimed 1,413 lives – paltry by comparison with the casualties on the Western front but sufficient to bring the war home to people in Britain. In reply, the British fliers killed 746 Germans in a total of 242 raids.

There was a school of thought which predicted dire consequences for Britain if it was the victim of a concerted air attack during the 1920s. But its voice was ignored by those who funnelled their thinking and their actions towards peace following the 'war to end all wars'.

Only when fighting broke out between China and Japan in 1931 and parts of Shanghai were reduced to rubble by Japanese bombers did air power come back on to the agenda.

Still, the British government at the lengthy international disarmament conference of 1931 urged that military and naval air forces be abolished. The conference ended inconclusively – but not until 1934, by which time Britain was substantially behind in the rearmament race. Italy had begun to build up its military, and Germany, now led by Hitler, was doing the same despite limitations still in force from the Treaty of Versailles.

Then it was left to the people who flew for thrills to make the running in air technology between the wars.

Racing became the pursuit of playboys, which not only earned them accolades and acclaim but won the infant industry some valuable knowledge. For example, the British Supermarine S.6 racing plane – which was a winner of the prestigious Schneider Cup – was transformed into the Spitfire fighter. In Germany, the Messerschmitt 109 set a speed record of almost 470 miles per hour in 1939 and went on to father some of the Reich's most effective planes.

Although flying speed increased, the overall performance of many aircraft did not, on account of the lack of fuel capacity. New faster-than-ever trips were inhibited by the number of stops necessary for re-fuelling. Greater capacity was needed to increase their range.

In 1935 the first B-17 Flying Fortress rolled onto the runway

Now it was the turn of the US to rise to the challenge. In 1935 the first B-17 Flying Fortress rolled on to the runway, with its ability to travel thousands of miles on one fuel tank. Meanwhile, the Douglas Aircraft Company unveiled the DC-3, with its top range of more than 2,000 miles. Both machines were winners.

Left: **A pilot hauls himself from the cockpit of his Beaufighter, this one equipped with radar.**
Right: **An Italian Macchi aircraft.**

Above: **By March 1936 an early version of the Spitfire – which was based on a racing seaplane – was flying, although it was modified before becoming a battle winner.**

Britain was seeing a revolution in air power of its own with the development at Rolls Royce of the PV-12 engine, the Merlin, in 1933. Aircraft manufacturers in 1935 had turned out the Hurricane, a stalwart fighter

In Germany the Luftwaffe was reborn on 26 February 1935 with a total of 1,888 aircraft

plane which even in those early days was capable of speeds of more than 300 miles per hour. In total, 12,780 were built in Britain and a further 1,451 in Canada.

The 1930s saw the development of radar in Britain, vital for both air and sea forces. After realising that aircraft interfered with radio signals, Sir Robert Watson-Watt of the National Physical Laboratory hit on radio detection and ranging, in which a travelling aircraft reflected a radio pulse and was thus visible on a screen linked to a radio receiver. Radar gave the Allies a vital leg-up during the opening phase of the conflict. Indeed, it took the Germans some time to understand how it was that their bomber and fighter formations so rarely escaped attack during the Battle of Britain. As the war progressed, radar was fitted to planes for use against aircraft carrying out night raids on Britain, providing at last an antidote to blitz bombers.

In Germany the Luftwaffe was reborn on 26 February 1935 with a total of 1,888 aircraft and 20,000 officers and men. Powering the new air force were four companies – Daimler-Benz, Junkers, BMW and Siemens-Halske. It was the designers from Daimler-Benz who dispensed with the carburettor and introduced a multi-point fuel-injection system, giving a pilot far greater control during rapid airborne manoeuvres. The rival Rolls Royce engine was prone to cutting out during dives.

BRITAIN LAGS

The arrival of the Luftwaffe caused consternation in Britain and was enough to spur the Air Ministry into action. New military aerodromes mushroomed on the east coast. Yet still there were crucial delays and hold-ups in the building of planes.

◆ EYE WITNESS ◆

Tony Langdon-Down joined the Royal Air Force in March 1941 when he was aged 18.

'I left school because the war started and began to read for the bar. As soon as I was 18 I joined the RAF – not for any particular desire to fly but I wanted to get into the services and there was a shortage of pilots.

For four months I was in Cambridge which is where I learnt to fly. Going solo for the first time was one of the highlights of my life. I completed my flying training and was operational by February 1942.

I was a defensive night fighter mostly serving with 219 Squadron. It was a tremendous way to grow up. After a few months I joined a Beaufighter squadron, flew out to Casablanca and from there we went to Algiers and Tunis. It was the first time I had been abroad.

We took part in the Sicily landings. I didn't see much action except for patrolling. When we returned to Britain, we left all our old planes to the Americans. They found them extremely difficult to fly.

I was an instructor when flying bombs started to fall. I volunteered to fly Tempests, single-seater night planes. The flying bombs came over on the back of Heinkels. I only shot down two. One blew up in my face which was rather unpleasant.

We didn't bring them down in built-up areas which made our job difficult. When they came to an end I rejoined a Mosquito squadron.

Although we did night flying we did tests on our aircraft in pairs during the day. I went out with another plane one day when it was very cloudy. We came down through the cloud and we were 500 feet over a port. The next minute all hell let loose. The port was Dunkirk where a pocket of German resistance remained. To my horror the other plane was shot down. We were hit but we were able to get back to Britain to land. The wife of one and the fiancée of another crew member were visiting the base for the weekend. Their deaths came as a terrible shock because there was no reason to suppose they were in any danger.

As the end of the war approached, my commanding officer asked me to make a small speech for VE day. I travelled to the BBC in London to record it. Sitting in the mess after Germany surrendered, we were listening to the radio when Princess Elizabeth made a short speech. It was followed by me. As you can imagine, there was uproar among my friends. I hardly recognised my own voice.

I didn't have a very glorious war. Flying wasn't the dangerous occupation when I joined that it had been. The main risk to me was my own flying ability. We did fly in some pretty fearsome conditions, though. I remember taking off in thick fog when I was chasing flying bombs and wondering how I would ever get down again.'

The Wellington bomber, designed by Sir Barnes Wallis, was prepared on paper by 1932. However, its first flight was not until June 1936 and it wasn't delivered for active service for a full two years after that.

Even as late as 1938 the Royal Air Force were woefully ill-equipped. Sir Maurice Dean, Private Secretary to the Chief of the Air Staff, pointed out: 'The re-equipment of Fighter Command had barely begun. The radar chain was half completed. Of the 45 fighter squadrons deemed necessary at the time, only 29 were mobilisable and all but five of these were obsolete. The five modern fighter squadrons could not fire their guns above 15,000 feet owing to freezing problems.'

The onset of hostilities did much to speed ahead technology and cast off caution.

When war broke out the pride of Britain's flying stock were Hurricances and Spitfires. However, there

Below: **German Messerschmitt 109s like this one caused plenty of headaches for Allied pilots.**

Above: **Boeing B-17 Flying Fortresses ready for action. The enormous capabilities of these classic aircraft were a tremendous boon to US airmen.**

> ***At sea, the slow Swordfish still earned their colours despite their advancing years***

were also Fairey Battles, Gloster Gladiators, and Bristol Blenheims, all hopelessly outdated. In September 1940 the first Bristol Beaufighters were introduced, complete with radar sets to combat night attackers. At sea there were slow Swordfish – which still earned their colours despite their advancing years, both in sinking the Bismarck and in the successful raid on the Italian fleet in Taranto.

During the war came the Handley-Page Halifax, which was progressively bettered, the subsequent Halifax Mark III, known for its versatility, and the heavy-duty Avro Lancaster. Best-loved of all was the wooden Mosquito, fast enough with its two engines to outrun many of its German adversaries on bombing runs.

ESCORT FIGHTERS

Ranged against them were Henschels, old-fashioned but nevertheless effective, the Ju.87 'Stuka', an ideal Blitzkrieg weapon thanks to its terrifying siren wail, Junkers, Heinkels, Dorniers and Messerschmitts. One of the most successful late arrivals in the German air fleet was the Focke-Wulf 190, which preyed on bombers. However, the Germans never found a successful formula for a heavy bomber, preferring instead fast bombers like Heinkels.

The best of Japan's aircraft were carrier-borne. They included the Mitsubishi A6M, better known as the Zero, torpedo-armed Nakajimas and dive-bombing Aichis. It came as a mighty shock, but the Japanese, when they entered the war, had the best air force in the world both in terms of agility and range.

◆ EYE WITNESS ◆

E. Rickman, who had been building model aeroplanes since he was a child, opted to join the Fleet Air Arm in April 1942. By 1944 he was based on HMS *Illustrious* and flew Grumman Avengers, US-made aircraft and the pride of the British fleet.

‘In January 1945 we were told the twin oil refineries at Palembang in Sumatra which provided the Japanese with nearly half the aviation fuel they needed in South East Asia had to be put out of action. One of the refineries was successfully bombed despite a barrage balloon protection. Three days later we were told the next one was our target.

During the briefing, our commanding officer Lieutenant-Commander Charles Mainprice, told us: “I consider this operation to be highly dangerous . . . I consider this strike to be so dangerous that if anyone would prefer not to fly, I shall respect his wishes and I shall not, repeat not, think any the less of him for so doing.”

The next day at about 4.45am as we approached Palembang, I could see the target ahead and the balloons. Just before I made our dive an enemy plane got on our tail. Suddenly, the Browning gun jammed. Fortunately, it was our turn to get in line for attack. I trimmed the Avenger for the dive and put the stick forward and the enemy plane broke off its engagement. There were three aircraft ahead of me. I could see one balloon cable between us and the pump house which was our prime target.

The commanding officer who went in first didn't see it. To my horror, he hit the cable with his port wing, cutting off two thirds of it as clean as a whistle. His plane went into a spin and exploded on impact seconds later.

The senior pilot next in line saw the cable and steered around it. But I could hardly believe my eyes when the third plane in line hit the same cable and suffered the same fate as the CO. I felt sick and angry but I didn't have too long to think.

It was my turn to go in. I went around the cable and met a huge smoke cloud which was obliterating the target. I had no choice but to go through it. The plane bucked in the turbulence and emerged from the smoke on its side at 500 feet.

I levelled out, went to tree-top level and headed around the coast, blasting away with my front guns at any target I could see.

On my way back I saw another Avenger which looked all right. But before my eyes I saw it descend into a shallow dive and blow up as it hit the sea.

At the end of the attack we were told there were 18 direct hits on the target and we did not need to return again.’

In their aircraft arsenal, the Americans had the invaluable Boeing B-17 Flying Fortress heavy bomber, and later the North American P-51 Mustang long-range escort fighter. On the other hand, they had problem planes, too. Captain Philip White was in a squadron of Brewster Buffaloes – heavy with armour plating and lightly armed – which was virtually wiped out by Japanese Zeros. He later wrote: ‘It is my belief that any commander who orders pilots out for combat in a Brewster should consider the pilot as lost before leaving the ground.’ The Australians who were given 154 Brewsters with which to defend Malaya. Within three months every one was destroyed.

A welcome addition to the US ranks during the war was the P-51 fighters, which had enough range to protect bombers on long-distance missions deep into Germany. In the bomber fleet, as well as Flying Fortresses, there were Liberators, less effective but with the supreme advantage that one rolled off the assembly line every 50 minutes back at the Ford Motor Company in Michigan.

LACK OF TACTICS

At the start of World War II, British tactics were virtually non-existent. Planes merely took off and headed in the general direction of their target. It was only when aircraft formations ascended in unison heading for a common target with the support of fighter escorts did the British find some success.

Throughout the war, aircraft design was refined to provide faster fighters and better bombers. The latters' capacity for bombs was continually increased. Also, aircraft which were ‘jacks-of-all-trades’, such

Aircraft design was refined to provide faster fighters and better bombers

as bombers that could act as transport planes or were able to fly low-level missions to drop supplies, were now in demand as aircraft began to take a broader role in the war.

Below: Sir Robert Watson-Watt was a pioneer of radar, which became crucial during World War II.

Fortunately for the Allies, the Luftwaffe fell into disfavour with Hitler and many new German innovations were scuppered. Nevertheless, Hitler maintained a lively interest – which ensured a financial lifeline – in the development of rockets and jets.

From test centres of the Third Reich came the ME-163 Komet, capable of speeds of 600 miles per hour. Still in its infancy, it did not cause the headaches for the Allies that it promised.

Its fuel was a combination of C-Stoff (hydrazine hydrate in methanol) and T-Stoff (hydrogen peroxide and stabilisers). When the two fuels were mixed they transformed into an explosive hot gas, sufficient to kill any members of the ground crew who accidentally combined the two on the ground.

Below: **The military version of the Douglas DC-3, the C-47, entered service during 1941. The aircraft was known as the Dakota in the RAF.**

Inside there were only five engine controls for the pilot to consider. These were off, idle and thrusts one, two and three. His mind was often taken away from the business of flying by the incredible agonies of extreme G-forces not to mention the high possibility of death by fire should the plane explode.

In fact, the Komet was too fast to be effective against the much slower Allied planes

After the flight came the hazardous and problematic landing, done in a gliding skid on the undercarriage. In fact, the Komet was too fast to be effective against the much slower Allied planes. Swooping down on Flying Fortresses, for example, the target was only in range momentarily before the Komet shot past. They also became targets themselves for Mustang fighters who took to patrolling near Komet bases to pick them off as they landed.

Britain was not far behind. Sir Frank Whittle, an RAF officer, piloted its first jet-propelled aircraft as early as May 1941 but Britain failed in the race against the Germans to get it into service.

DEATH RAY

There were other ideas being knocked around in Britain which failed to come to fruition. One, originating in World War I, was to freeze the clouds and mount gun emplacements on them. Another was to freeze stretches of sea and use them as landing strips – which was a project taken seriously enough to be given a code-name, 'Habbakuk'. Thirdly, there was the much-loved idea of the death ray. No matter how hard scientists tried, they found it only worked when the chosen victims had first been thoroughly poisoned.

Despite the odd flight of fancy, aviation science and skills moved on

Above: **The Junkers Ju.87 'Stuka' dive-bomber was a terrifying aircraft.**

apace on both sides during World War II. However, it can be assumed that the Germans were a step ahead of the Allied countries as far as technology was concerned. Many

Many German scientists were enticed to America...many on a 'no questions asked' basis

German scientists were enticed to America following the war, many of them on a 'no questions asked' basis. There was an outcry years later when it was discovered that people regarded by some as war criminals were harboured in the US.

◆ EYE WITNESS ◆

Hilda Richards, from Cardiff, Wales, joined the ATS in 1941 when she was 21 and worked on the radar which guided one of the biggest 'ack-ack' guns in London.

❛There were only three gun sites like us in the country. One was on Wimbledon Common, one in Regent's Park and ours was outside Eltham. Most guns measured 3.5 while this had a 5.25 specification. It came from an abandoned cruiser.

I was one of six girls on radar. I still keep in contact with four of them. There was a lot of comradeship. For most of us it was our first time away from home. I wouldn't have missed it for anything – even when we counted 108 buzz bombs passing over us in just one night.

We worked any time the sirens went off at a post about 100 yards away from the gun itself. Rotas were 24 hours on duty, 24 hours on standby and 24 hours off. It sounds tough but we got used to it.

If we were on standby we could get some rest until we heard the siren. Then we would slip our trousers and battledress over our army pyjamas and run. The majority of us smoked because we had to keep awake.

We were tracking in south east London and on the edge of the Kent fields on circular radar screens. We could recognise the Germans as our own used to carry a signal. Then we could take height, distance and bearing and relay these to the command post.

I can remember when Hitler's rockets came down. They didn't make a sound. They would land and two houses would suddenly be gone. Every man and woman who wasn't doing anything would run to pull people out. It was just an unwritten law.

Looking over towards Woolwich one night, I saw all the huge oil drums on fire after an air raid. It was like daylight even though it was miles away.

I was in London, my sister came to join me and my brother went over to Burma. I never even considered what my mother went through at the time until I had children of my own.❜

FIRES IN THE NIGHT

While German bombers were pounding Britain during 1940 and 1941, the British people huddled night after night in stuffy, cramped shelters and comforted themselves that Royal Air Force bombers were delivering similar punishment to the citizens of the Third Reich.

Sadly, they were mistaken. While British bomber crews were full of sterling young men with an iron resolve, their success rate in the first half of the war was low – and for very sound reasons.

Night bombing was far safer for the aircraft and crew, as the Germans had illustrated in their raids over London. RAF Bomber Command was keen to conserve these valuable assets too and favoured night-time bombing raids instead of exposing its forces to daylight risks.

But the Luftwaffe was operating from occupied airfields a short hop over the English Channel. For the Royal Air Force to strike at the heart of Germany, its pilots and planes had to fly many more miles than their German counterparts, in aircraft that were ill-equipped for long-distance flying or bombing. It took time and investment for new, heavier bombers to be commissioned for the task.

The already limited resources of Bomber Command were also stretched in many different directions. Not only were there the demands of bombing raids over enemy territory but Coastal Command was in constant need of planes to combat the U-boat menace in the Battle of the Atlantic. With Britain under threat of isolation and annihilation if the U-boat peril was not seen to, the need to have planes available for maritime duties was paramount in 1940. In addition, the Middle East and North Africa required a complement of bombers, together with crews and parts – all of which required regular replacements. For a while, night bombing raids over Germany were abandoned altogether so the force could focus on its duties elsewhere.

EARLY PROBLEMS

Operational shortcomings put the Royal Air Force at a disadvantage, too. For the first sorties were flown, rather informally, on an almost individual level. Following a joint briefing, each aircraft would depart at five-minute intervals following a course chosen by its own navigator to the target. Often, the crews would not catch sight of another plane until after their return. Given that each would offload its bombs over a wide area, the effect of single bomb drops on the ground were, of course, much less than an orchestrated raid involving greater numbers.

For a while night bombing raids over Germany were abandoned altogether

Added to this, the navigational aids available on planes at the time were wildly inaccurate. Crews conforming to their instructions were sure their bombs were away right on top of the targets. It was not the case. While bomber crews scored hits on clear nights in easily located target areas, bombs dropped on blacked-out Germany or on targets shrouded with industrial haze as often as not fell short. After the war it was discovered that 49 per cent of the ordnance released by the British crews between May 1940 and May 1941 exploded in open countryside.

Navigators used maps, a sextant and a procedure of 'dead-reckoning' to work out their position, all of which could be fouled up by poor weather conditions. It meant that precision bombing by the RAF at night could be successful only on clear, bright, windless nights of which

Left: **German planes on a daylight raid of London before night-time tactics were introduced.** ***Far left:*** **The Renault works at Billancourt after bombing by the Allies.**

Above: **A Wellington bomber and its crew pepare for an arduous night's work over HItler's 'Fortress Europe'.**

there were precious few. Once again, it took many months before the difficulties of finding targets under cover of darkness were resolved.

Bomber Command was continuing to sustain losses from the missions over Germany, in exchange for precious few results. It soon became clear a new tactic was in order.

The principles of precision bombing – a technique almost impossible to execute successfully given the constraints of the era – were abandoned for 'area bombing'. For this, not only was the target itself carefully chosen but also its neighbourhood. Thus a large factory producing vital components in the middle of open countryside would be overlooked in favour of a smaller factory among other small factories and industrial workers' housing.

That way enormous damage could be caused for the same amount of effort and risk as was required in precision bombing. It gave a twofold purpose to bombing missions. Not only was there the clear-cut intention of halting Germany's industrial output but, in addition, the chance to demoralise the people by bringing the war to their doorstep, making them homeless or otherwise hampering their daily existence.

The concept was fostered by Air Marshal Sir Richard Peirse, in charge of Bomber Command during 1941. Unfortunately, the failure of his forces to destroy three German warships, Scharnhorst, Gneisenau and the heavy cruiser Prinz Eugen, while they were in dock at Brest, northern France, did little to enhance the ebbing reputation of the force.

BREST RAIDS

While these three sea monsters roamed, the British suffered terribly. Between them they were responsible for the loss of HMS Glorious, HMS Ardent, HMS Acasta as well as the armed merchant cruiser Rawalpindi and something in the order of 115,600 tons of merchant shipping.

EYE WITNESS

David Greig, of the Royal Australian Air Force, was 19 and second pilot on a Wellington bomber when his aircraft was shot down in a night raid over Germany.

"We were already on fire when a night fighter pounced on us. My heart was in my mouth. I knew the situation was grim. We were facing death, that's all there was to it. I saw a piece of shell come out of nowhere and it hit me. I was furious that a German had wounded me and scared at the same time. I was knocked out for a moment. When I came to, I was by the rear escape hatch. The flames had really taken a hold now. The smell was acrid. Mechanically, I clipped on my parachute. Then another crewman shoved me out. I was injured in the arm and chest.

The Germans had no trouble capturing me. The pain was both mental and physical. I felt I had not much longer to live."

In the spring of 1941, Bomber Command flew 1,161 sorties against the ships, scoring just four direct hits, none of which caused substantial damage. All this for the loss of 43 bombers. Even when the three ships left the dockyard to slip back to

Below: **Air Chief Marshal Sir Arthur 'Bomber' Harris, commander of the RAF's Bomber Command.**

home ports, the 242 planes sent to destroy them as they sailed failed to dent the pride of the German navy.

It signalled the departure of Peirse and the arrival of Air Chief Marshal Arthur Harris, who adopted the idea of area bombing as his own.

Afterwards, Harris summed up his position. 'I had to prove, and prove quickly, to the satisfaction of those who mattered that the bomber force could do its work if it was large enough and if its efforts were not frittered away on objectives other than German industry as a whole.'

The historic town was engulfed in a firestorm which swallowed up 200 acres

His first priority was to bolster the stocks of planes available to carry out attacks, particularly heavy bombers of which there were fewer than 70 when he arrived.

An opportunity to prove the ability of himself and his men came just a matter of weeks after he was installed at Bomber Command. On 3 March 1942, Harris sent a force of 235 bombers across to Billancourt, France, where a giant Renault factory was turning out tank components for the German war effort.

The planes set off in three waves and now Harris mimicked a successful German tactic. The first wave carried not only bombs but a large number of flares which would light up the target for subsequent attackers. With the River Seine acting as a brilliant marker, 223 of the aircraft found their targets within the space of two hours. This concentrated attack had the desired effect. Enough machinery was put out of action to stop the factory working for several months. As a happy spin-off, many completed products were wrecked.

SUICIDE BOMBERS

Germany formed its own squadron of suicide bombers known as the Sonderkommando Elbe. They first went into action in April 1945 and engineered mid-air collisions with laden Allied bombers. The 300 volunteers were told they could parachute to safety if possible.

It appeared to Harris that Bomber Command had received the change of fortune it so urgently required. With a new directional aids now in use among navigators, he felt that Germany's industrial heartland of the Ruhr was his for the taking.

Five days after the Renault raid, 211 bombers took off and headed towards the city of Essen. Once again, the technique of using flares and incendiaries was employed. But this time, many had burnt out before the second wave of bombers had got the measure of the area. It finally bore the hallmarks of the haphazard raids which Bomber Command were now known for. Another three attacks made on ensuing nights also failed to produce the spectacular results Harris yearned for although there was widespread damage caused in the city.

Harris had to wait until the end of the month for the next feather in his cap, a raid carried out against Lübeck, a Baltic port comprising many ancient timbered buildings.

When almost 200 aircraft dropped 300 tons of high explosives plus 144 tons of incendiaries on the night of 28/29 March, the historic town was engulfed in a firestorm which swallowed up 200 acres.

ROSTOCK RAID

At the end of April another Baltic port, Rostock, was given similar treatment. The targets for the bombers were specifically a factory which produced the Heinkel 111 aircraft and in general the town itself. An estimated 70 per cent of the old town was turned to rubble with direct hits being scored against the factory too. Of the 168 bombers that set off for the mission, all but 12 returned safely.

Harris noted with satisfaction that, yard for yard, the destruction wrought in Germany by Bomber Command in those two raids equalled that caused by the Luftwaffe in Britain in 1940 and 1941.

Below: **The Renault works at Billancourt was destroyed after Bomber Command was fired with fresh resolve.**

The Nazi hierarchy was riled by the savage encroachment into the Fatherland. In a fury, Hitler ordered raids against Britain's historic cities to even the score. He picked the targets from a tourists' book of Britain called the Baedeker Guide. Among them were Bath and Exeter.

'MILLENIUM'

For one daring raid against a factory producing U-boat parts, Harris was persuaded to return to daylight attack. New Avro Lancaster heavy bombers were brought in for the assault on Augsburg in southern Germany. Together with their fighter escorts they flew in low over enemy territory to avoid radar detection and then began a breathtaking roof-top scrap with Luftwaffe fighters before hitting their target. The cost was high. Seven out of 12 bombers were lost. The crews of the returning battle-scarred aircraft were decorated for their bravery.

It confirmed the general view that daylight raids were unacceptably risky given the aircraft available. In any event, Harris became far too preoccupied with his latest tactical trailblazer to consider further daylight sorties. The continued all-out efforts to obliterate the Ruhr were proving frustrating. With the lack of truly efficient navigation and the industrial smog it was impossible to co-ordinate a successful mission. He had pondered long and hard about pulling off a single operation which would earn the admiration of those doubters at home and the trepidation of the Germans.

The answer, he decided, was a thousand-bomber raid against a prime target in Germany. But, given that the most he had been able to rally for an attack to date was 235 bombers, it seemed this was nothing more than a flight of fancy. That was until Harris's deputy Air Vice Marshal Saundby got to work.

With the use of borrowed aircraft from Coastal Command and the entire stock of his reserves flown by trainee pilots and instructors alongside existing crews, it was conceivable that 1,000 bombers could be summoned for an epic raid.

Code-named 'Operation Millenium', the first thousand-bomber raid took place against Cologne on 30 May 1942. All the planes were to strike within an hour and a half.

The raid represented a new departure in aerial warfare. The largest force of aircraft dispatched to Britain at any one time had numbered 487 while the British had never been able to gather together more than 235 bombers at any one time.

Churchill himself was captivated by the idea of such a mighty strike. He

Below: **An RAF Wellington bomber is loaded with bombs before setting off on another mission.**

was under pressure from fellow politicians who saw the largely inconclusive night raids against Germany as a waste of time and effort. Stalin was also waiting in the wings, always demanding a decisive attack by the British against Germany. It was realised that there would be too few German fighters in the air to halt the impact of the raid. The possiblity of collision was to be diminished by dividing the planes into three groups operating in parallel lines against different targets. Despite the immense commitment, it seemed the risks were calculated. The raid could not end up as the swansong of Bomber Command.

Ground crews worked flat out on damaged aircraft to furnish Harris with the required number

1,046 BOMBERS

For a while, 'Operation Millenium' appeared under threat when Coastal Command refused to release the 250 planes it had promised. Its chiefs had got cold feet. They decided the risk of releasing their aircraft was too great. Saundby was left scraping the barrel to fill the ranks for the raid. A spell of poor weather which caused the operation to be postponed proved a saving grace. Ground crews worked flat out on damaged aircraft to furnish Harris with the required number. On the morning of 30 May the magic 1,000 was surpassed.

The 1,046 bombers departed from 53 airfields across Britain and assembled in a 70-mile convoy across the North Sea. Before them went 50 fighter planes ready to duel with the defending Luftwaffe.

Mechanical difficulties accounted for 100 planes in the force even before it had reached the target and they turned back to base.

Still, the first bombs and incendiaries were dropped at 12.47am on 31 May. The rest of the operation went according to plan. Land-based defences and intercepting Luftwaffe fighters were overwhelmed and the last bomber dropped its load over Cologne at 2.25am.

As they flew homewards, rear gunners could see the city burning from 150 miles away. The night's work destroyed 18,432 buildings, killed nearly 500 people, injured 5,000 more and rendered almost 60,000 homeless. Forty bombers did not return, which meant the loss of 40 instructors and 49 pupils.

Above: **Sir Barnes Wallis, inventor of the bouncing bomb, which proved a huge morale-booster in Britain.**

At home it was hailed as a triumph. Yet the success in itself put pressure on Harris to produce more of the same. Now the British public expected many more raids of similar dimensions to lambast the enemy.

An attack against Essen on 1 June involving 956 bombers failed to achieve the same degree of destruction. Key industrial centres escaped from the raid unscathed.

It wasn't until 25 June that another large-scale attack was attempted, this time against Bremen. Poor weather once again hindered the 1,006 bombers as they sought their targets. It was a resounding success except for the higher number of casualties claimed by Germany. This time 49 aircraft didn't come home.

The Luftwaffe, in charge of ground defences as well as airborne, quickly realised the intention of Bomber Command. Now it set about denying the British an opportunity to hammer German industry.

To combat the upsurge in Luftwaffe fighters and improve the success of the night bombing raids, a

EYE WITNESS

Dennis Golding, of Gosport, near Portsmouth, England, was a British rifleman with the King's Royal Rifle Corps. As a light infantryman he was engaged in hand-to-hand combat with German troops throughout the 1944 advance across Western Europe.

"On VE day we marched into Hamburg to find everything devastated except the roads. The Germans had cleared them and stacked up all the re-usable bricks they could salvage. It was typical German efficiency and I suppose it also helped improve their morale.

The civilians were more or less glad to see us. There was certainly no hostility and, like our own people, they were just glad it was all over. We weren't allowed to fraternise with them at first. If you were caught you were put on a charge. That rule soon broke down. When they spoke to you you felt you had to talk back."

Pathfinder force was created. In charge was Australian Group Captain D.C.T. Bennett, a first-class pilot and skilled navigator.

Their aim was to fly 'finder' aircraft over the target on parallel tracks two miles apart dropping flares, creating a 'runway'. Behind them came 'illuminator' aircraft, dropping further flares picking out the target area precisely. Then came the 'marker' group which started fires with incendiaries to pinpoint the targets for following bombers. When it was cloudy the Pathfinders dropped 'sky-markers', parachute flares which lit up the target beneath the cloud cover. In response the Germans used fires on the ground as decoys in much the same way as the British did during the Battle of Britain. The Pathfinders proved a massive boon to the night bombing raids, with the additional attraction that their loss rate was a smaller-than-average three per cent.

The Air Ministry favoured a plan to knock out three giant dams

At the end of 1942 Bomber Command diverted resources to the 'Torch' landings in North Africa and provided valuable support. At the same time it carried out some successful raids over Italy, finding the air defences there far lighter than those in Germany.

Still, Harris was determined to kill off German industry in the Ruhr. By March 1943 he was set upon a concerted attack on the region. The Battle of the Ruhr got underway on the night of 5 March with a 442 aircraft raid and continued for six weeks more or less relentlessly. During the battle the famous Dambusters raid was carried out. Although Harris himself was opposed to it, the Air Ministry favoured a plan to knock out three giant dams which would deprive the region of vital hydroelectric power. To do it, Wing Commander Guy Gibson and his squadron had to drop new 'bouncing bombs', designed by engineer Barnes Wallis.

Above: **A Lancaster of 617 Squadron, loaded with its 'bouncing bomb' before heading for the German dams.**

DAMBUSTERS

Each bomb weighed five tons, measured five feet in length and four feet across. Carried in a special cradle beneath a Lancaster bomber, it went into action with backspin imparted, which would cause it to skip along the surface of the water until it met the dam wall.

The targeted dams – the Möhne, the Eder and the Sorpe – were 150 feet high and their concrete walls were almost the same again in thickness. The skill required by Gibson and his crews was enormous. They had to fly in at low altitude to evade German radar and drop their bombs at precisely 60 feet above the water and exactly 425 yards from the perimeter of the dam.

On the night of 16 May 1943 the 19 Lancasters took off in three waves. In the first wave of nine planes, headed by Gibson, one plane was lost to flak and several bombs went astray before three explosions ripped through the Möhne Dam and a flood poured down the valley.

In the second wave just one of the five Lancasters reached the Sorpe Dam, under the guidance of Flight Lieutenant McCarthy, an American serving with the RAF. His bomb load damaged the dam but failed to breach it. Meanwhile, the third wave scythed a gap in the Eder Dam.

Eight of the Lancasters together with their 56 crew members failed to return. And, although it was a feat of undoubted heroism, the damage took the Germans just three months to repair. Perhaps it was most successful in capturing the public's imagination

◆ EYE WITNESS ◆

George Funnell joined the 55th Kent Regiment in 1939 aged 17, after lying about his age. He witnessed the Blitz in London when he was stationed at an anti-aircraft battery – and later saw the destruction caused by air raids in Germany after fighting his way through Normandy, Belgium and Holland to Hamburg in 1944.

‘In Hamburg there was mile after mile of devastation. I lived through the London bombing but it was nothing like as bad as that over Germany.

Even when we got to Hamburg, long after the air raids had taken place, there was still the stench of death coming from crumbled buildings. It took ages to find some of the buried remains.

On the streets we only found a few old men and young boys. The rest of the male population had been called up into the army. The vast majority of the people we met were women struggling to survive as best they could.’

in terms of a morale-boosting coup and depriving the Atlantic Wall in northern France of some labour. This was redirected instead to the Ruhr to repair the damage there.

Harris returned to his bombing campaign, this time picking Hamburg as the target for prolonged attack . ‘Operation Gomorrah’ began on 24 July with the first use of aluminium foil. It had been known for years that a simple device like this would fog the German radar screens. But the Air Ministry held back from using it in case that same device was used in retaliation. In fact, Germany was well-acquainted with the technique and also refrained from using it, for the same reason. Called ‘Window’, it was brought in to play on the orders of Churchill in a bid to counter the Luftwaffe defences.

■ HAMBURG HORROR ■

At midnight 740 bombers dropped 92 million strips of tin foil, creating the desired effect. The planes went on to deliver almost 3,000 tons of bombs. Subsequent attacks made by night and day virtually unremittingly devastated the city's defences. Fine weather had left the city dry as paper. As new fires were sparked by existing blazes, the perpetual heating of the air which funnelled into the sky caused a firestorm, akin to a tornado with wind speeds of 150 miles per hour. Delayed detonators on some of the bombs wrought havoc among the rescue workers as they attempted to deal with the blazes.

The melting temperatures achieved in the raid scorched buildings and bomb shelters, water mains and electric cables. Hamburg endured the horror for nine days by which time ten square miles of the city was laid waste. In total 2,630 bombers unleashed more than 4,300 tons of incendiaries and a similar amount of high explosives, creating in total three firestorms. The death toll was an estimated 42,000.

Harris continued to work through the list of German cities he hoped to destroy. His armoury now included a 12,000lb bomb and some excellent new nagivational aids and target-finders. Now his sights turned towards Berlin. The German capital was a far-distant target from British airfields across hostile territory. The Battle of Berlin opened in November 1943 and a further 15 attacks were launched against it. Although the demands on the participating crews of Bomber Command were eased when airfields were opened in Europe following D-Day, those raids cost no less than 587 aircraft together with 3,640 men killed or missing. When reconnaissance photographs proved little was being gained from the attacks, they were suspended.

If Harris hoped to end the war with his tactics bathed in a blaze of glory, he was disappointed. At last, public opinion both in Britain and overseas began to question the wisdom of saturation bombing. (The phrase ‘terror bombing’ was constantly rebuffed by air chiefs.)

On 30 March 1944 a night raid by Halifaxes and Lancasters was sent awry by a strong wind which sent them into the arms of defending Luftwaffe fighters. Out of the 795 aircraft that set off, 95 failed to return and another dozen crashed in England. Night bombing raids afterwards came to an end.

Below: **A reconnaissance photograph reveals the damage done to the Möhne Dam by Wing Commander Guy Gibson and his Dambusters.**

CARRIERS AND KAMIKAZES

Americans were down in the dumps following the raid on Pearl Harbor. With the Imperial Japanese Army and Navy riding roughshod over the Pacific and South East Asia, there was no glimmer of optimism as the nation became preoccupied with the sight of its young men marching off to war.

Finally, on 18 April 1942, there came some small consolation for the folks back home. It was provided by a daring air raid into the heart of Japan itself. American airman Lt-Colonel Jimmy Doolittle, a veteran of glamorous pre-war air races, delivered a small but significant strike back against the aggressor.

The newly commissioned aircraft carrier Hornet, bearing 16 army bombers, in the company of fellow carrier Enterprise and a body of cruisers set off from Midway Island towards Japan. Some 650 miles short of the Japanese coastline, the fleet stopped so the B-25s could be launched. Despite the stiff wind, the planes took off at dawn, heading for Tokyo and other major cities.

At noon, 13 of the aircraft unloaded their cargoes of bombs over Tokyo. The other three dropped incendiaries on Nagoya, Osaka and Kobe. In fact, little was achieved in the exploit and many Japanese people remained unaware that it had even taken place at all. Its main effect was to shock the Japanese commanders who had until now considered themselves somewhat impregnable.

It now seemed vital to the Japanese to take control of Midway Island, a gap in the extended front line they had created in the Pacific. Those who doubted the wisdom of pushing Japanese lines still further were persuaded that the vulnerability of the home islands warranted the new push.

As for the attacking American B-25s, they did not have the range to return to the aircraft carriers which were by now high-tailing it for home. Their orders were to seek out friendly airstrips in China.

JAPANESE REPRISALS

All made it out of Japanese air space without a problem although one crash-landed in Russian Vladivostok. Only four of the planes actually touched down while the rest ditched after their crews baled out. Three of the men were captured by Japanese troops operating in China and shot. A further five died but 72, aided by Chinese peasants, made their way to Chungking and eventual freedom.

The most terrible effects of the raid were probably felt by the Chinese. When Japan realised the escape route taken by the fliers, troops exacted revenge against the native Chinese, slaughtering anyone suspected of aiding the airmen.

It was some 30 months before Japan was once again in range of American bombers. This time the aircraft were far more fearsome, their capacity for wreaking terror much greater than in 1942.

Even from airfields in India and China in the summer of 1944, the American fliers found it difficult to carry out effective missions over Japan. The only island within their range was Kyushu, the southernmost Japanese home island.

At noon, 13 of the aircraft unloaded their cargoes of bombs over Tokyo

It took victory in Saipan, freeing the Marianas Islands and their airfields, before a more comprehensive bombing campaign could begin. On 24 November 1944 110 B-29s took off with the aim of knocking out Japan's aircraft industry in Tokyo, Nagoya, Kobe and Osaka. They were to do it by dropping 500lb bombs from high altitudes. But cloud cover obscured the targets and at the end of it, only one factory out of nine had been struck.

Left: **Lieutenant-Colonel Doolittle ties a medal to a bomb bound for Japan.**
Far left: **US Navy pilots receive a final briefing before a raid on Tokyo.**

Left: **A B-25 heavy bomber takes off from the USS *Hornet* to deliver its load to Japan. The Doolittle Raid sparked Japanese reprisals in China.**

At the start of 1945 Major-General Curtis LeMay was brought into 21st Bomber Command. He had an inkling that the flimsy wooden shacks which filled Japanese cities were a major fire hazard. He pinpointed incendiaries as the best weapon with which to attack them.

On 4 February his theories were proved right when a force of 70 Boeing B-29 Superfortresses dropped 160 tons of incendiaries on the centre of Kobe. A tenth of a square mile was burnt out and that included several factories.

The ploy was repeated on 25 February, this time against Tokyo. Now 172 B-29s dropped nearly 450 tons of incendiaries, devastating a square mile. An estimated 28,000 buildings were razed.

To add to the effect of the bombs, a fresh wind fanned the flames

Interrupted by the call for aid in Okinawa, LeMay had time to consider his options. The use of incendiaries had proved itself beyond question but the effect was far more widespread when the bombs were dropped from lower altitudes. It pointed to the need for night raids.

In advance, a single plane would pinpoint targets with marker bombs and the rest of the bombing party would follow at intervals of every couple of minutes.

On the night of 9 March 334 B-29s took off and showered a 12-square-mile industrial area of Tokyo with 1,700 tons of oil incendiaries. To add to the effect of the bombs, a fresh wind fanned the flames until it seemed the entire city was on fire.

RAIDS CONTINUE

Anti-aircraft fire claimed 14 of the planes but their mission was an outstanding success. No less than 16 square miles of the city had been burned out, with 267,000 buildings flattened and 84,000 people killed. An official Japanese report noted: 'People were unable to escape. They were found later piled upon the

Right: **Kobe, Japan's sixth-largest city, comes under attack with incendiaries dropped by US B-29s. Fires have already been sparked in the industrial areas.**

◆ EYE WITNESS ◆

Masuo Kato was a reporter in Japan throughout the war and detailed the terror by fire inflicted by US bombers.

'For more than three years my small nephew Kozo Ishikawa, who was about five years old when the war began, held an unshakeable faith in Japanese victory. To his small world it was unthinkable that the Emperor's armies could suffer defeat or that the Japanese navy should endure any fate other than glorious victory.

After his home was burned to the ground during a B-29 raid, destroying almost every familiar material thing that had made up his existence, he told me with great gravity: "We cannot beat the B-29." The psychological effect of the loss of his home went deep. He had been one of the happiest and most carefree of children. He became thoughtful and serious and it was seldom that he laughed. He became ill and died shortly after the war was over. A nervous breakdown, the doctor called it.

The B-29s had brought the war to the Japanese people in a real and personal sense and each man had begun to form his own opinion on whether Japan was winning or losing. My nephew's experience was repeated many thousands of times in every part of Japan. To each family that watched its home and belongings go skyward in a rush of smoke and flame, the news from Okinawa, true or false, meant little. For them, their personal war was already lost.'

bridges, roads and in the canals. We were instructed to report on actual conditions. Most of us were unable to do this because of horrifying conditions beyond imagination.'

Two nights later 285 aircraft dropped 1,800 tons of incendiaries at Nagoya. Without the wind, the fires were more contained. One aircraft was lost and two square miles of the city laid to ruin.

On 13 March Osaka was the target for 274 B-29s. About 13,000 people died, 135,000 homes were

Below: **A large area of Osaka was levelled by sustained fire-bomb attacks carried out by the Americans.**

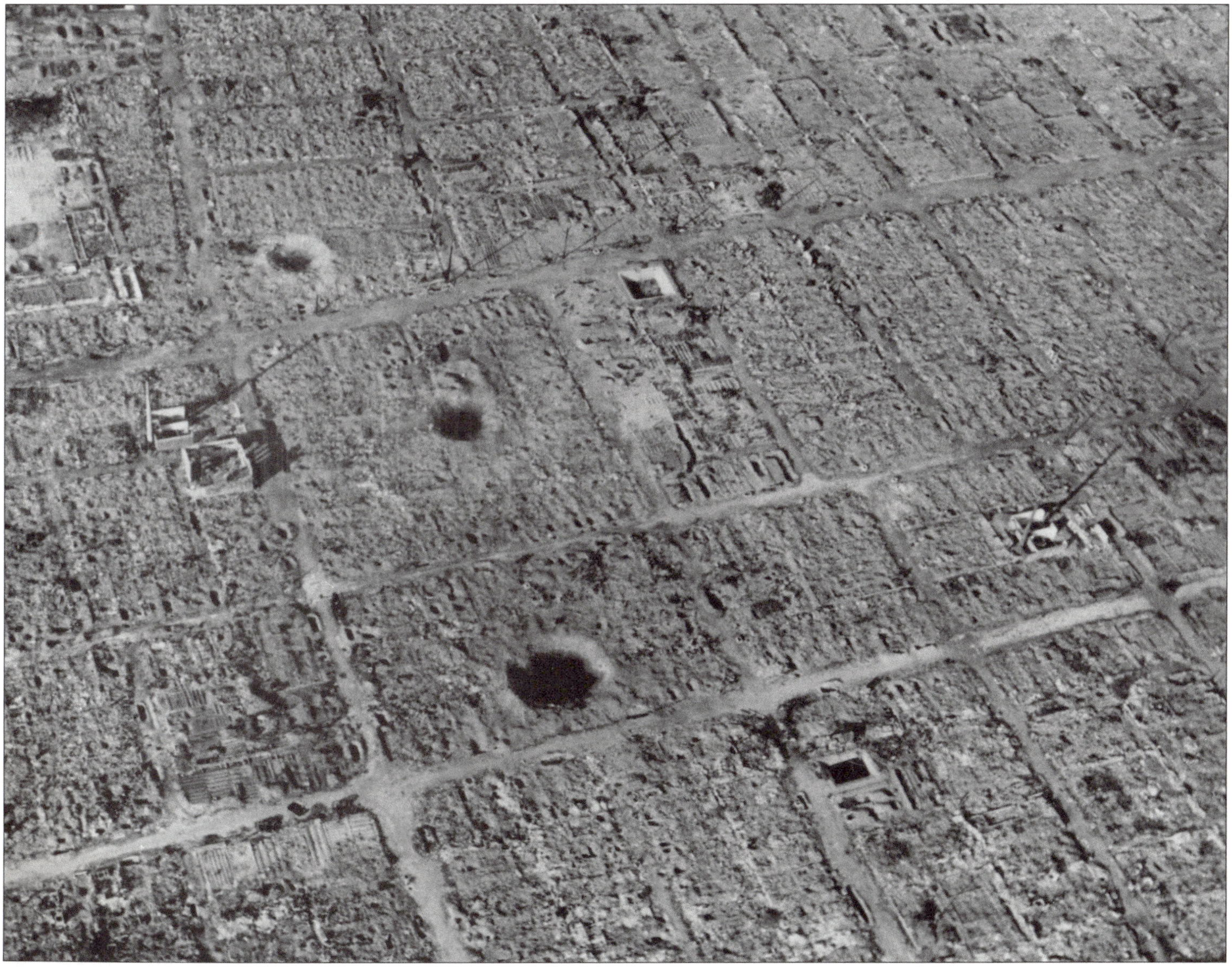

Above: **Tokyo became a patchwork city following the destruction delivered by the incendiary raids, with much of its industry and housing flattened.**

burned down and 119 factories were knocked out. Once again, the American losses were light, with just two aircraft lost and 13 damaged by anti-aircraft fire.

The heaviest attack yet was made against Kobe on 16 March, this time using 2,355 tons of mixed oil and thermite bombs. More than 300 planes launched the onslaught and three were lost, an outstanding one per cent loss rate. At Kobe 2,669 people were killed, with 66,000 houses and 500 industrial centres eradicated. A fifth strike was made against Nagoya three days later, in which high-explosive bombs were among those used.

In 11 days 21st Bomber Command had notched up 1,595 sorties and dropped more than 9,000 tons of incendiary bombs, proving that Japan was exposed to complete devastation. As important to the Americans was the low level of losses the bomber command had sustained. Only 20 aircraft were destroyed, mostly by anti-aircraft fire and only one per cent of the crews had been lost.

The rate of attacks was kept up, some made by day but all those against the heavily fortified Tokyo were at night. In the summer bad weather hampered the airmen but still they rained fire on the major Japanese cities, week in, week out. When these had all been substantially ruined, LeMay turned his planes' attention to the secondary Japanese cities.

LEAFLETS DROPPED

Now he became involved in psychological warfare, too, with the dropping of thousands of leaflets prior to the raids, naming 12 cities which were going to be hit and urging the civilian population to evacuate. Not only did this spread confusion but helped to demoralise the battered, war-weary population.

At the same time, 21st Bomber Command was involved in a mine-laying programme to complete the blockade of Japan. Between the end of March and the middle of August about 12,000 mines were dropped into the waters around the islands. It meant that in May mines were responsible for more losses to Japanese shipping than submarines were.

Submarines were then able to move into the Sea of Japan, looking for the occasional ship which had escaped the blockade and organising lightning sabotage raids.

Right: **Major-General Curtis LeMay (left) believed the policies of 21st Bomber Command – the obliteration of key centres – would bring about Japan's defeat.**

◆ EYE WITNESS ◆

Geoff Michael, from Perth, was 18 when he joined the Royal Australian Air Force in 1942 and trained under the Empire Air Training Scheme, launched in 1939 to train Allied pilots. He went on to complete 32 missions with Bomber Command and retired from the RAAF after 37 years' service, as Air Commodore.

"Even though it was a hectic and sad time, one is inclined to remember most of the good things – the great time I had on leaves etc.

But I also recall vividly having my aircraft shot up by ground fire and fighters. The fortunate part was that I was never wounded and never lost a crew member.

However, I did lose a close mate who was killed in a daylight raid over Germany. I saw the plane go down but didn't realise at the time it was my mate's plane.

It was a time when we were conditioned to death. Every morning you expected not to see the next one. So all you did was to read the operations board, see if you had been rostered on a missions and, if your weren't, go out and relax and have a good time."

With the Japanese Imperial Navy now completely impotent and the majority of surviving Japanese aircraft in hiding, American aircraft carriers also sailed close to the home islands, their aircraft launching attacks at regular intervals. Freed by the end of the war in Europe, Royal Navy warships joined the US Navy in the waters off Japan, and combined attacks were launched, before the typhoon season made air attack impossible.

In August a Japanese plan to launch 2,000 kamikaze planes on the 21st Bomber Command bases in the Marianas was discovered. The carrier fleets moved to within range of the airfields on the northern island of Honshu where the heavily camouflaged planes were being gathered for the covert operation. For the first time since the end of the Okinawa campaign, a Japanese fighter counter-attacked and a kamikaze aircraft struck an American destroyer. Still, the Japanese airfields came in for heavy bombing.

DEVASTATION

In Japan itself the people were enduring appalling hardship. Homelessness caused by the effective incendiary strikes left many in dire straits. If their factories had also been destroyed they were in an even worse situation. There were few building materials on hand in the devastated city and little food. Inadequate rice rations were sometimes being boosted by sawdust. The wounded were also receiving scant attention. But if the population went to the countryside to scavenge food where it could, who would man the remaining factories and workplaces?

By August, Japanese ministers had called for a collection of acorns to turn into food

Natural disasters, including extensive flooding, added to their problems. By July 1945 an estimated 25 per cent of all housing in Japan had been destroyed, leaving 22 million people without a roof over their heads.

By August, Japanese ministers had called for a collection of acorns to turn into food. Yet despite their difficulties, the people spoke of surrender only in whispers. An inherent will to serve the Emperor prevented an uprising. The Japanese would struggle on regardless.

LeMay was delighted with the success of his aerial bombing campaign and was convinced that it alone would bring Japan to the point of surrender. His confidence was somewhat premature.

DAYLIGHT RAIDING

By the time America entered the war, the British had some fixed ideas about aerial combat.

The Royal Air Force had learned the hard way that aircraft employed on daylight raids were more vulnerable to the enemy, that bombers had a better survival rate when they were accompanied by fighters. Harris and the other British air supremos thought it best that the US fliers reinforced the existing night bombing expeditions being carried out by the RAF.

Novices at warfare in the air they may have been, but the Americans had thoughts of their own on the issue. US pilots were untrained for night missions. Not only that, they had a different bombing philosophy from that of their British counterparts, that of precision bombing.

FIRST ACTION

Given that their Flying Fortresses were, in their opinion, well defended and that the aircraft were equipped with a revolutionary new bombsight called the Norden which 'could drop a bomb into a pickle barrel from 20,000ft', it was their preferred plan to fly during the day. No amount of friendly persuasion from the British could dissuade the US air chiefs from their stated aims.

The Royal Air Force held Flying Fortresses in low regard. During experiments with the new aircraft in 1941, pilots felt they became large targets for German defences. For their part, the US air chiefs believed the RAF had used the Fortresses wrongly, sending them out in twos and threes instead of in a large formation when they performed best.

First taste of action for the US pilots came on 17 August 1942 when a dozen Flying Fortresses flew out of Grafton Underwood aerodrome, heading for Rouen, northern France.

With protection from four squadrons of RAF Spitfires, they made the flight, dropped the 18.5 tons of bombs on railway targets and returned home intact but for slight damage on two Fortresses caused by flak.

On the mission was Ira C. Eaker, a brigadier-general, and superb pilot, who set up the headquarters for the US 8th Air Force in Britain and was soon given command of its European flight operations.

There followed a succession of small-scale bombing raids. The success of precision bombing was trumpeted by Eaker although, like the number of victories claimed against the Luftwaffe on such outings, the statistics had to be treated with caution. Nevertheless, in 13 missions, just two planes were lost – an enviable record.

The Norden bombsight 'could drop a bomb into a pickle barrel from 20,000 ft'

Still, their operations had been strictly 'local' on missions regarded as workaday 'milk runs' by the British pilots.

Left: **A US Flying Fortress carries out a daylight bombing raid over Germany.** ***Below:*** **By the middle of 1942, US aircraft were a familiar sight in Britain.**

***Above:* US B-17s plough on towards their targets while fighter escorts fend off marauding enemy interceptors. The range of escorts increased during the war.**

Then poor weather began to not only hamper the efficiency of the Norden bombsight – which had earned its colours in the cloudless skies above New Mexico and frankly struggled in the cloud- and smog-filled heavens above Germany – but brought about the wholesale cancellation of planned raids.

Like the RAF, the USAAF had to do its bit for the 'Torch' landings in North Africa in late 1942, which cut aircraft and crew stocks by a third.

Then the Luftwaffe hit on a new tactic which took its toll among the American fighters. Canny German pilots spotted the Achilles heel of the Flying Fortresses, which was head-on attack. There were no defences on the nose of the plane and the Germans had enough guts to mount daring frontal assaults despite the obvious risk of collision. It appeared that the 8th Air Force, clinging to its belief in daylight raids, was on a hiding to nothing.

Churchill was among those who strongly objected to the Americans going their own way. He believed that precision bombing being executed by the Americans, which needed daylight to succeed, was the height of folly. Area bombing under the cover of darkness appeared a far better bet and might encourage the Americans to venture for the first time over German territory.

At the Casablanca Conference of January 1943, the British leader was hoping to persuade Roosevelt that daylight bombing raids should be dropped in favour of night bombing operations by both air forces.

Eaker had one chance beforehand to convince Churchill otherwise. Finally, it only took one sentence. His proposal in favour of the continuation of daylight raids contained the words: 'By bombing the devils around the clock we can prevent the German defenses from getting any rest.' The idea instantly caught Churchill's imagination. He vowed to give Eaker the opportunity to prove his point.

THE B-24 ARRIVES

Afterwards there came the Casablanca Directive, backing orchestrated day- and night-time bombing raids and listing top targets, namely centres of German industry.

On 27 January that year the US airmen were at last sent to Germany to produce the goods. Their target was Wilhelmshaven on the North Sea, where U-boats were made. By now B-24 Liberators had joined the Flying Fortresses in the ranks. Of the 53 which left for Wilhelmshaven, three were lost and the remainder had to battle at close quarters with Luftwaffe fighters while achieving only moderate success in their mission. The difficulties of daylight raids over hostile territory were crystallised for the Americans.

Danger from flak and enemy fighters was not the only problem faced by the Americans on their daylight raids. To stay out of reach of the enemy, they flew at high altitudes, usually above 20,000 feet. The chill of the air

Area bombing under cover of darkness appeared a far better bet

numbed their faces, crammed as they were in small cockpits. Tension mixed with boredom as another lengthy mission got underway. For a while each member of the crew remained vigilant for the enemy, but there were long hours when the Luftwaffe didn't

◆ EYE WITNESS ◆

Burdsall D. Miller, from Sacramento, California, joined the US Army Air Force, aged 24, following the Japanese raid on Pearl Harbor. Based in Sudbury, England, he became a colonel and flew 32 missions.

❛ I flew ten missions in a B-24 Liberator and then switched to B-17s for a further 22 raids. Most of them were daylight raids over Germany although we also hit Italy and Norway. I got shot up but never enough to bale out or crash land.

As command pilot, I sat in the co-pilot's seat and made all the decisions as far as the group or squadron were concerned that day. I was scared but I was trained to do a job. The thing that made the biggest impression on me was flying in formation and seeing a wing man shot down in flames. It was very upsetting.

But we all got fatalistic and figured when our time came we were going to get it. Perhaps that made us seem like we had nerves of steel. Otherwise we would not have lasted. We had some men who didn't last. They refused to fly, but it was very few out of a considerable number of men.

As soon as we dropped our bombs we got out of the target area as most were heavily defended. As we turned we could see bombs hitting and we could usually tell if we had hit the target.

I have a big picture at home. It was taken on a raid over Germany on one of the most heavily defended targets. We had turned to start our bombing run. We just opened our bomb bay doors. To the left of us, another plane was doing the same when some flak went right into the bomb bay. The plane just exploded. Nobody got out alive. At the moment the plane blew up, my waist gunner took the picture. ❜

appear in which there was little to do but study the clouds.

Every US airman wore a steel chain vest to protect himself from flak. His flight suit was thick to protect him from the cold. Each wore a parachute and an oxygen mask, itself deeply uncomfortable. Despite the elaborate precautions, there was at least a one in ten chance of dying.

Americans adopted different flying patterns to suit the daylight nature of the raid. Up to 21 planes would form a box which was staggered both vertically and horizontally for protection. Three boxes lined up in the air to form a combat wing.

To improve the accuracy of bombing, the most skilful men were placed in the lead planes and gave the signal for the rest of the aircraft in the box to drop their bombs.

> ***Historically the US Army Air Corps was treated as the poor relation by the White House***

On the ground, Eaker had his own problems. Historically, the US Army Air Corps, as it was first known, was treated as the poor relation by the White House. Priorities changed only slowly during the war and Eaker spent many fruitless hours harrying his bosses in America for extra planes and crews. It wasn't until mid-1943 that his efforts paid off. The US 8th Air Force could at last increase the size and effectiveness of its attacks.

DANGEROUS GAME

Perhaps the biggest bonus of all to the US airmen was when fighter aircraft increased their range, although it was late in the conflict when a combat aircraft which could escort bombers into the heart of Germany and back came into use.

Daylight missions were stepped up in 1943 and the heavy bombers recorded some admirable successes. Assisting their cause was the decision to scale down Luftwaffe defences in France by withdrawing two groups back to the Reich to improve air security there. The Allies were now

Left: **Despite damage from a German rocket in the Battle of Berlin, this US B-17 still managed to land safely.**

Above: **A German tank factory is ruined and its new stock in tatters following a daylight raid by the United States Army Air Forces. The Americans specialised in precision bombing by day.**

making a concerted effort to draw the Luftwaffe aircraft into the sky at every available opportunity, trying to shoot down as many as possible. Of course, a considerable number of Allied planes fell victim while playing this dangerous game.

PLOESTI RAID

The US medium bombers fared less fortunately. A flight of B-26C Marauders which set off from Great Saling on 17 May was virtually wiped out during a raid on Haarlem.

And raids later in the year proved yet again the perils of daylight raiding. On 1 August 1943 the target was Ploesti, the oilfields in Romania which fed Germany's war machine. The Americans had planned a surprise attack, keeping radio silence and flying at low altitudes to avoid radar detection. Their approach was to be over a lightly defended sector and their escape route was to North Africa. Alas, the planes were picked up in Germany as soon as they left the runway. Navigational errors brought them in over the thickest of the anti-aircraft gunfire. Fifty three of the Liberators on the raid were shot down in enemy territory. A further 55 reached Libya in such appalling condition that they were fit only for scrap. The results were disappointing, too, with only a small dent being made in the oil production levels.

In the same month, the Americans tackled Regensburg and Schweinfurt, key centres for aircraft manufacture and the production of that tiny but indispensible engineering component, the ball bearing. The raids would be without fighter escorts. So deep were the targets inside Reich territory the existing fighters did not have the capacity to fly there and back.

The German pilots were under no illusions. They were no longer the favoured elite

When the 146 Flying Fortresses dispatched for Regensburg crossed the German border they met a hail of fire from a host of defending Luftwaffe planes. The German pilots were under no illusions. They were no longer the favoured elite. Hitler was once again frustrated at the lack of success brought home by the Luftwaffe which once had seemed invincible. Now fewer resources than ever were being ploughed into aircraft manufacture and the training of crews. Without this investment, the entire force would surely be strangled. Luftwaffe production chief Ernst Udet had already committed suicide in despair at the plight of the force. The pressure was on to prove the worth of the air force before the unpredictable Führer sought his own revenge against it.

Those Flying Fortresses that survived the arduous 90 minutes to Regensburg dropped their bomb loads and made off in haste towards Algiers, saving themselves a possibly fatal return journey.

Now it was the turn of 230 Flying Fortresses to run the gauntlet across Germany en route to Schweinfurt.

The fierce firepower of 300 Luftwaffe fighters battered and buffeted the American planes. While the Germans lost 25 fighters that day, the US bombers were down by 60 and another 47 were so badly damaged they could not be salvaged.

The figures were bleak for the USAAF. In October 1943, 153 aircraft were lost in a single week. It led to the halt of bombing raids without fighter escort.

DROP TANKS

Fortunately the drop tank appeared, a suspended fuel tank which could be jettisoned when empty. This was attached beneath the wing to vastly increase the range of fighters. Hot on its heels came the P-51 Mustang, a fighter with an 850-mile range. It helped tip the balance of the air war over Europe in favour of the Allies.

By 1944 the Allies were producing twice the number of aircraft as the Reich was. The Luftwaffe's difficulties were compounded by the damage each fighter was sustaining which wasn't being repaired. Hitler was punishing the disappointing Luftwaffe by depriving it of essential materials to stay alive.

Yet the theories adopted by 'Bomber' Harris for the RAF and Eaker for the USAAF cannot be said to have been an outright success. Harris hoped to defeat the Third Reich by saturation bombing, destroying the will of the German people. The question of the morality of carpet- bombing civilian centres, including the ancient city of Dresden late in the war, raged long after the conflict had ended.

Eaker targeted industrial centres, certain that concerted bombing raids would cause Hitler's regime to topple. Despite the bravery and commitment of the pilots, the principles were flawed. In fact, Hitler illustrated only too well over Britain in 1940 that air power by itself was not sufficient to win a war. Bombs from above failed to break the will of the Germans in just the same way as they had failed to crack the British. And damage sustained by industry could inevitably be repaired – particularly in Germany with the use of forced labour.

The liberation of Europe came with the arrival of the ground troops, albeit with priceless assistance from their colleagues in the air forces.

EYE WITNESS

Lieutenant Harmon Cropsey, a former state senator from Decatur, Michigan, served with VB110, a US Navy squadron, navigating Liberators on 12-hour anti-submarine patrols into the North Atlantic. He was based at Dunkeswell in Devon under RAF Coastal Command.

"One of my fellow officers was Joe Kennedy, John's elder brother. We used to meet quite regularly in the mess and swap notes. He was flying the same aircraft as me.

It was Joe who volunteered for one of the most dangerous missions of the war. The idea was to strip everything out of one of the Liberators and pack it full of TNT. He was to fly this out over the North Sea to a prearranged navigational point and bale out. The plane would then be radio controlled to crash-land on its target – a 40-foot layer of reinforced concrete around some U-boat pens in Holland.

But something went wrong and the plane exploded in mid-air over England. We never found out what the problem was, and obviously there was nothing left of his body. He was a very brave man.

Our base lost an awful lot of airmen. The other two squadrons, 103 and 105, had around two-thirds of their crews killed in the first few months of our arrival in 1943. There was a German advanced training base at Brest and they were sending up the twin-engined Junkers 88 which had a 50-knot advantage on our planes. If you got caught out over the sea on a clear day you were a dead duck. Your only hope was to find cloud cover.

I know of only one plane, flown by a Free Czech crew, which made it home after being attacked. We were just fatalistic about it.

Every mission you were handed a top secret chart showing where all the Allied subs and ships were supposed to be. It was absolutely vital. One day I'd got this thing spread out inside the plane with the door still open. Suddenly the engines start and the whole thing blows right out into a field. I go haring after it and my flight suit gets caught on some barbed wire. As a result, I fall and dislocate my shoulder.

That really extended my war. You were allowed to go home after 25 missions but because of my injury I stayed behind when all my chums left. Then they decided they needed an experienced navigator to show the new crews what to do. I ended up flying 42 missions."

Hitler was punishing the disappointing Luftwaffe by depriving it of essential materials

THE ULTIMATE WEAPON

In Japan, the people were preparing for all-out war against invading Americans.

As early as November 1944 all Japanese men aged between 14 and 61 were conscripted. Women between the ages of 17 and 41 were on standby for military service, too. This new militia was being schooled in beach defences and guerrilla warfare. Those that were left unarmed – the vast majority – were told to practise martial arts skills as a form of defence. The message from the rulers of Japan was to be seen on giant posters hung around towns and villages. 'One hundred million will die for Emperor and nation!'

Key installations in Japan had been destroyed by the American bombing campaign. Much of the Japanese shipping had been sunk already by US ships, aircraft and submarines, which were now operating a tight blockade of the island coastlines. Japan was being starved of everything she needed to survive – yet still there was no sign of surrender.

In fact, various feelers had been extended by the Japanese through Swedish and other neutral sources for a negotiated peace, all cloaked in secrecy. Finally, the Japanese foreign ministry approached Russia to act as an intermediary, partly in a bid to divert Stalin from opening another battlefront with the war-weary country. But Japanese demands were unacceptable to the Allies who would agree to nothing less than an unconditional surrender.

Not for the first time, the lack of a cohesive war leader in Japan was keenly felt. Emperor Hirohito was a figurehead who could apparently do little without the say-so of his government. Prime minister Admiral Suzuki was eager to sue for peace but there still remained in opposition hardliners who were willing to fight to the death. No one, it seemed, was in outright control and nobody dared utter the word 'surrender' without the prospect of assassination, political retribution or military uprising looming large. So Japan struggled on as best it could in a vacuum of indecision.

The losses among the American troops in the landings around the Pacific islands had horrified and shocked the commanders. By now painfully aware of the Japanese resilience to attack and reluctance to surrender, they viewed invasion of the home islands as a tall order. The estimates for the number of US casualties appeared virtually open ended.

Later Truman confided that America had developed a new bomb which could end the war

When Truman met with Churchill and Stalin in Potsdam in July 1945, they discussed the inadequate peace overtures from the Land of the Rising Sun. Later Truman confided that America had developed a new bomb which could finally end the war.

ATOMIC POWER

He was referring to the end result of the Manhattan Project, begun back in 1942, in which a band of elite scientists, the most admired brains of the free world, had got together to probe the possibilities of atomic power.

By December of that year, the scientists under the leadership of Professor Enrico Fermi made a significant breakthrough in understanding how to spark a man-made chain reaction.

At two big plants – Oak Ridge, Tennessee, and Hanford, Washington – work continued in the bid to extract the essential substance known as U-235 from uranium for the manufacture of plutonium.

It wasn't until 5.50am on 16 July 1945 that the theory was finally put into full-scale practice. In the scorched sands of the New Mexican

Far left: **Scientists knew they had created the ultimate weapon when it was tested.** ***Left:*** **Truman confided in Churchill about the bomb at Potsdam.**

Above: A weapon similar to that detonated at Nagasaki. Its weight was 10,000 pounds and it was equivalent in power to 20,000 tons of TNT.

Below: Dr Albert Einstein (left) was the initial innovator. Dr Robert Oppenheimer (right) took up his theories and made them reality.

desert the plutonium bomb called 'Fat Man' was detonated. (It won the name by having a passing resemblance in profile to Churchill.) Observing scientists could barely hide their awe at the intense power man had created.

Dr Robert J. Oppenheimer, the physicist directing the project, instantly realised the shattering effect it would have on the world.

TRUMAN INFORMED

A telegram detailing the precise results of the 'Fat Man' experiment was sent to the Potsdam Conference for the consumption of President Truman – who himself had only found out in April the full scope of the Manhattan Project.

Two further atomic bombs were made and dispatched to the Pacific while the politicians pondered. Was the world ready for the atomic age? Once unleashed, would this mighty new force return to act as a Sword of

Observing scientists could barely hide their awe at the intense power man had created

Damocles poised over the heads of free and fair countries?

Churchill for one was in no doubt that it should be used. Afterwards, he wrote: 'To avert a vast, indefinite butchery, to bring the war to an end, to give peace to the world, to lay healing hands upon its tortured peoples by a manifestation of overwhelming power at the cost of a few explosions seemed, after all our toils and perils, a miracle of development.

'British consent in principle to the use of the weapon had been given on 4 July, before the test had taken place. The final decision now lay in the main with President Truman, who had the weapon. But I never doubted what it would be nor have I ever doubted since that he was right.'

In his memoirs, Truman wrote: 'Let there be no mistake about it. I regarded the bomb as a military weapon and never had any doubt that it should be used.'

Still, there was debate about whether Japan should be warned about its terrible fate. A chain of events finally overtook these talks.

The Potsdam Conference finally closed on 26 July with an ultimatum for Japan. It called for unconditional surrender. In the absence of such a surrender, Japan would face complete destruction. Just two days later Premier Suzuki announced his country would be ignoring the Allied threat.

Such belligerence was enough to confirm an order sent to Lieutenant-General Spaatz, commanding general of the US Army Strategic Air Forces to prepare a B-29 to carry the newly fabricated atomic bomb.

Below: **Smoke rises more than 60,000 feet into the air following the explosion of the atomic bomb at Nagasaki.**

◆ EYE WITNESS ◆

Dr Michihiko Hachiya was at home when the first atomic bomb – 'Little Boy' – fell on Hiroshima from the bomb bay of B-29 'Enola Gay'. He recalls the moment of impact in his eye witness account *Hiroshima Diary*.

‘The hour was early, the morning still warm and beautiful. Shimmering leaves reflecting sunlight from a cloudless sky made a pleasant contrast with shadows in my garden as I gazed absently through wide-flung doors opening to the south.

Clad in vest and pants, I was sprawled on the living room floor exhausted because I had just spent a sleepless night on duty as an air raid warden in my hospital.

Suddenly a strong flash of light startled me – and then another. So well does one recall little things that I remember vividly how a stone lantern in the garden became brilliantly lit and I debated whether this light was caused by a magnesium flare or sparks from a passing tram.

Garden shadows disappeared. The view where a moment before all had been so bright and sunny was now dark and hazy. Through swirling dust I could barely discern a wooden column that had supported one corner of my house. It was leaning crazily and the roof sagged dangerously.

Moving instinctively, I tried to escape but rubble and fallen timbers barred the way. By picking my way cautiously I managed to reach the roka and stepped down into my garden. A profound weakness overcame me so I stopped to regain my strength. To my surprise, I discovered that I was completely naked. How odd. Where were my vest and pants. What had happened?

All over the right side of my body I was cut and bleeding. A large splinter was protruding from a mangled wound in my thigh and something warm trickled into my mouth. My cheek was torn, I discovered, as I felt it gingerly with the lower lip laid wide open. Embedded in my neck was a sizeable fragment of glass which I matter-of-factly dislodged and with the detachment of one stunned and shocked I studied it and my blood-stained hand.’

Left: **Colonel Paul Tibbets, pilot of 'Enola Gay', waves from his cockpit before take-off on his epoch-making mission on 6 August 1945.**

On 6 August 1945 the first atomic bomb, called 'Little Boy', was released over Hiroshima. A mammoth 120 inches long and weighing 9,000 pounds, beneath its shell it contained the power equivalent to 20,000 tons of TNT. It was carried to its target in a B-29 called 'Enola Gay' which took off from the Marianas. In command was Colonel Paul Tibbets.

The uranium bomb exploded 2,000 feet above the centre of Hiroshima. Four square miles of the city was instantly wiped out. Those at the epicentre of the bomb were reduced to ashes along with buildings and cars. Beyond that immediate area, many more died and tens of thousands were horribly burned.

SHOCK WAVES

The authorities could only estimate the numbers of people who had perished in the ferocious cauldron. The final figure was put between 70,000 and 80,000 persons.

Colonel Tibbets later described how his plane was shaken by the shock waves as it sped away and told of the scene of devastation he left behind: 'There was the mushroom cloud growing up and we watched it blossom. And down below it the thing reminded me more of a boiling pot of tar than any other description I can give it. It was black and boiling underneath with a steam haze on the top of it. And, of course, we had seen the city when we went in and there was nothing to see when we came back.'

On 8 August further pressure was exerted on Japan when the Soviet Union declared war and launched an invasion of Manchuria.

'We had seen the city when we went in and there was nothing to see when we came back'

A day later a further atomic bomb dropped, this time on Nagasaki. It came from the bowels of another B-29, this one christened 'Great Artist', under the command of Major Charles Sweeney. About 40,000 people died this time with a further 60,000 injured.

It is doubtful whether the introduction of atomic weapons had a huge effect on the people of Japan. The scale and horror of the previous bombing campaigns had claimed victims by the thousand and caused acres of destruction. Wholesale killing, burns and homelessness was nothing new for them. The only fresh aspect was the radiation sickness spread among the survivors, the wide-ranging effects of which were not immediately apparent.

For the rest of the world, the double bombing was like a macabre sideshow

◆ EYE WITNESS ◆

Tsutomu Yamaguchi worked in the Hiroshima yard of the Mitsubishi shipbuilding company and was on his way to work when the bomb dropped more than a mile away.

‘Suddenly there was a flash like the lighting of a huge magnesium flare. As I prostrated myself there came a terrific explosion. I was lifted two feet from the ground and I felt a strong wind pass my body.

How long I lay in the road dazed, I don't know, but when I opened my eyes it was so dark all around me that I couldn't see a thing. It was as if it had suddenly become midnight in the heat of the day. When my eyes adjusted to the darkness I perceived that I was enveloped in an endless cloud of dust so thick it was black.

As the dust blew away and my surroundings became visible I saw what seemed to be thousands of tiny, flickering lamps all over the street and in the fields. They were little circles of flame, each about the size of a doughnut. Myriads of them were hanging on the leaves of the potato plants.

I looked toward the city and saw a huge, mushroom-shaped cloud rising high into the sky. It was an immense evil-looking pillar. It seemed to be reflecting every shade in the spectrum turning first one colour then another.

Feeling terribly weak and suffering intense pain from the deep burns on my face and arm, I stumbled into the potato field. There was a big tree out in the field and I headed for that. Sometimes I could only crawl, creeping from bush to bush. When I finally reached the tree I had no more strength to go on. And I had acquired a terrible thirst.

I saw a group of teenage boys unclothed except for torn underpants. As the boys came near I saw that they were pale and shaking severely. I had never seen such a horrifying sights as those five shivering boys. Blood was pouring in streams from deep cuts all over their bodies mingling with their perspiration and their skin was burned deep red like the colour of cooked lobsters.

At first it seemed strangely that their burned and lacerated backs and chests were growing green grass. The I saw that hundreds of blades of sharp grass had been driven deep into their flesh, evidently by the force of the blast.’

with people riveted by the footage and photos of the vast mushrooming cloud that rose up some 20,000 feet as the bomb was detonated.

JAPAN SURRENDERS

In any event, it was clear that Truman's pledge to ‘obliterate’ Japan was no empty threat. Hirohito himself was sickened at the sight of the suffering among his people. Finally, he found the leverage inside his government to bring the conflict to an end.

The day after Nagasaki was bombed, Japan broadcast a willingness to surrender ‘on the understanding that it does not comprise any demand which prejudices the prerogatives of the Emperor as Sovereign ruler.’

Yet still the hawks in the regime dragged their feet. A flight of US Navy carrier-borne planes flew over Japan on 13 August dropping leaflets spelling out the surrender so the people would understand that it was all over.

The following day at 11pm the Emperor himself told his people the war was over

The following day at 11pm the Emperor himself told his people the war was over. Even at this late stage, 1,000 militant soldiers stormed the Imperial Palace in a bid to prevent the surrender. They were beaten off by the Emperor's own guard.

VJ day was then declared on 15 August. The pockets of Japanese resistance around the Pacific and

***Left:* The atomic bomb scarred the landscape of Nagasaki so deeply it was beyond recognition.**

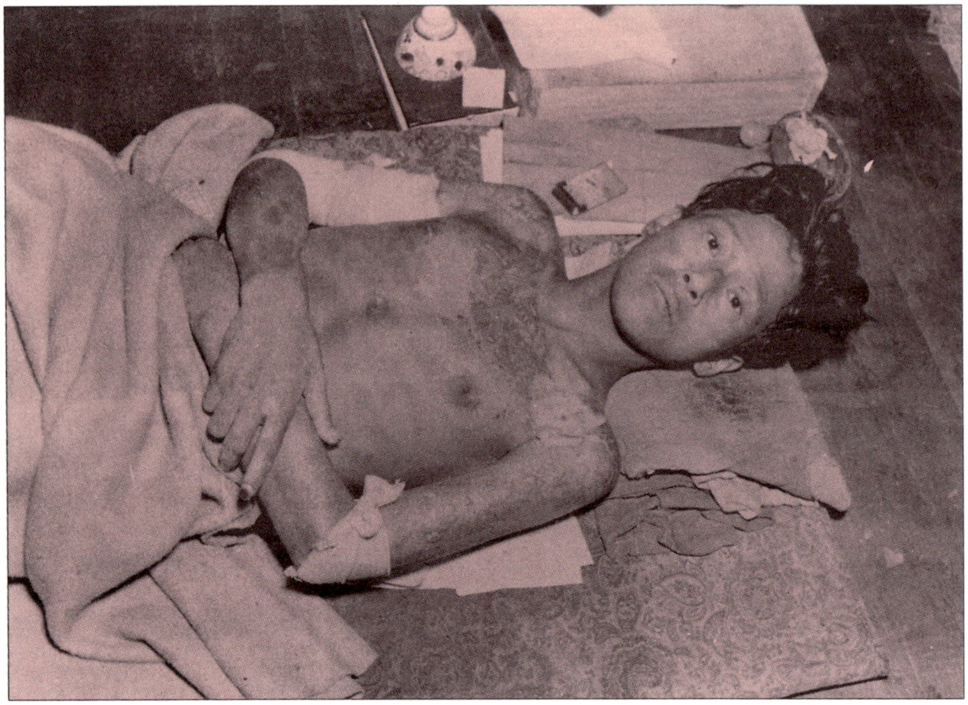

Left: **The luckier victims of the atomic bomb blasts suffered burns to their bodies. The remains of many of the victims were never found.**

South East Asia surrendered through the following month, ending with Hong Kong on 16 September.

In the meantime the official ceremony marking the outbreak of peace came on 2 September aboard the USS Missouri in Tokyo Bay. The Japanese delegation was led by the one-legged foreign minister Mamoru Shigemitsu, who wore a top hat for the occasion. The military wing of the country was represented by General Yoshijiro Umezu. There to receive them were dignitaries from all the countries that had taken part in the war against Japan – America, Britain, Australia, New Zealand, Canada, China, France and Holland.

'Let us pray that peace be now restored to the world'

Sailors squeezed into every available inch of the deck to witness the historic moment.

After the signing was over, General MacArthur gave a stirring speech opening the door to a new order.

'We are gathered here, representatives of the major warring powers, to conclude a solemn agreement whereby peace may be restored. The issues involving divergent ideals and ideologies have been determined on the battlefields of the world and hence are not for our discussion or debate.

PRAYER FOR PEACE

'Nor is it for us here to meet representing as we do a majority of the people of the earth in a spirit of distrust, malice or hatred. But rather it is for us both victors and vanquished to serve, committing all our peoples unreservedly to faithful compliance with the understandings they are here formally to assume. It is my earnest hope... that from this solemn occasion a better world shall emerge... a world dedicated to the dignity of man... Let us pray that peace be now restored to the world and that God will preserve it always.'

Right: **Servicemen greeted news of the atomic explosions with relief. The blasts probably saved thousands of US troops.**